STANDING
MY GROUND

HARRY DUNN
WITH
RON HARRIS

STANDING
MY GROUND

A CAPITOL

POLICE OFFICER'S

FIGHT *for*

ACCOUNTABILITY

and GOOD TROUBLE

AFTER JANUARY 6TH

hachette
BOOKS

NEW YORK

Hachette Books
Hachette Book Group
1290 Avenue of the Americas
New York, NY 10104
HachetteBooks.com
Twitter.com/HachetteBooks
Instagram.com/HachetteBooks

First Edition: October 2023

Published by Hachette Books, an imprint of Hachette Book Group, Inc. The Hachette Books name and logo are trademarks of the Hachette Book Group.

The Hachette Speakers Bureau provides a wide range of authors for speaking events. To find out more, visit hachettespeakersbureau.com or email HachetteSpeakers@hbgusa.com.

Books by Hachette Books may be purchased in bulk for business, educational, or promotional use. For information, please contact your local bookseller or email the Hachette Book Group Special Markets Department at Special.Markets@hbgusa.com.

The publisher is not responsible for websites (or their content) that are not owned by the publisher.

Library of Congress Cataloging-in-Publication Data

Names: Dunn, Harry (Police officer), author. | Harris, Ron (Journalism professor), contributor.
Title: Standing my ground: a Capitol police officer's fight for accountability and good trouble after January 6th / Harry Dunn; with Ron Harris.
Description: First edition. | New York, NY: Hachette Books, 2023.
Identifiers: LCCN 2023024764 | ISBN 9780306831133 (hardcover) | ISBN 9780306831140 (trade paperback) | ISBN 9780306831157 (ebook)
Subjects: LCSH: Dunn, Harry (Police officer) | Capitol Riot, Washington, D.C., 2021—Personal narratives. | United States. Capitol Police—Biography. | Police—Washington (D.C.)—Biography. | Presidents—United States—Election—2020. | United States—Politics and government—2017–2021.
Classification: LCC E915 .D86 2023 | DDC 973.933092 [B]—dc23/eng/20230612
LC record available at https://lccn.loc.gov/2023024764

ISBNs: 978-0-306-83113-3 (hardcover); 978-0-306-83115-7 (ebook)

Printed in the United States of America

LSC-C

Printing 1, 2023

I am one of the few recognizable faces and voices from January 6th. I dedicate this book to the men and women who answered the inconceivable call of duty and public service that day, whose voices, faces, and names you may never know.

*Get in good trouble, necessary trouble, and redeem
the soul of America.*

—John Lewis

CONTENTS

STANDING
MY GROUND

PROLOGUE

We need to talk about our trauma.

Yes, you and me.

You may not think you are experiencing it, but you are. Ask yourself, What has this nation been arguing over for the past two years? What conversation has been dominating the media and the government, occupying our courts and our daily conversations, and even separating friends and families? What is the subject we promise ourselves to avoid with strangers?

January 6, 2021. That's what the dictionary says trauma is—"a deeply distressing or disturbing experience."

Trust me. I looked it up.

The ripples from that day still threaten our democracy. The lives of election workers, the backbone of our electoral systems, are being threatened online via hundreds of messages on Facebook, Twitter, and Instagram by those who would disrupt our elections. "Watch your back." "I know where you sleep." "Be afraid. Be very afraid." Because I speak out about these challenges to our democracy, I get the same threatening messages. "We know where you live."

Domestic terrorists have shot out the electrical power systems for neighborhoods, and they are threatening to do the same for entire cities. Representatives in Congress continue to lie and claim our election system is rigged. Yes, we are still struggling with that day.

The only difference between your January 6th trauma and mine is where we were when we experienced it.

I was at the Capitol, immersed in a profane mix of sweat, screams, shrieks, anger, fear, blood, death, broken limbs, spit, hatred, horror, racism, bigotry, and heroism. Capitol and DC police officers fought hand-to-hand. Many of us thought we were going to die. Some of us did. We were cursed; doused with bear and pepper spray; and beaten with sticks, pipes, batons, shields, bike racks, and even the American flag.

Donald Trump, then the nation's commander-in-chief, did nothing to help us for three hours, even after politicians, his friends, and his own children begged him to. Instead, Capitol and Washington, DC, police officers battled alone. We fought for our lives, the lives of fellow officers, and the nation's elected leaders. It didn't matter if they were Republican. We didn't care if they were Democrat or Independent. They were the men and women we sent to Washington to govern our nation. It was our duty to protect them and our democracy.

We could have run away. We could have said, "We didn't sign up for this." But we did sign up for it—we just never imagined it like that. Hundreds of Capitol and DC police officers are still working through the physical and emotional scars of that day. All of us have changed. Some of us, physically, can no longer do the job. Others are haunted daily by what happened, including me. I still struggle with PTSD, post-traumatic stress disorder.

But as I tell you about my struggle that day, I want you to remember this. While I'm one of the officers whose job it was to protect the Capitol, like you, I'm first an American citizen who cares about this country and wants to see it do right. I'm a voter. I'm a taxpaying citizen. This is my country, and I deserve to know the truth to make sure this doesn't happen again.

We all do.

Just like I was marked by that day, you were too. You glared at your TV screen or listened to your radio in disbelief. You felt something you had never felt before, the shock and fear that somebody was trying to take over your country.

You and I had seen lots of demonstrations before at the nation's Capitol, many of them much bigger than this one—the original March on Washington for Jobs and Freedom in 1963, Veterans for Peace, the Million Man March, the Women's March on Washington, pro-choice rallies, antiabortion demonstrations, gun control, gun rights. Every issue you can think of from gay rights to immigration to climate change to the minimum wage to saving the whales.

Americans with different agendas have been coming to the Capitol for more than 150 years to tell their elected leaders what's on their minds. It is my job and the job of my fellow officers to protect them, no matter what their agenda.

We are Americans, and, as Americans, we have those rights. Freedom of speech. Freedom of assembly. This is not Iran or Russia or Venezuela. This is not one of those countries where citizens are beaten, shot, killed, or disappeared for expressing their beliefs, their desires, or their dissatisfaction.

But, this time, you were shocked because what you saw is not what Americans do. You looked on as thousands of Americans tried to kill or maim hundreds of other Americans. So-called American patriots brutally beat the men and women in blue they claimed to hold in such high regard. "Protect the Blue," they preached. "Blue Lives Matter."

They did this so they could get inside to attack our elected officials. They wanted to "Hang Mike Pence," or

"Drag that motherfucker through the streets." Another said she and her friend "were looking for [House Speaker Nancy] Pelosi to shoot her in the friggin' brain."

They said they were there to stop the will of the people and halt our 224-year history of the peaceful transfer of power. These weren't the international thugs and foreign terrorists of the movies trying to take over our country. Instead, these were people from our own communities—store owners, clerks, waiters, doctors, lawyers, IT specialists, real estate agents, CEOs, veterans and service members, police officers, accountants, retirees, and construction workers. Thousands of them screaming, spitting hate, and all with allegiance to one man: Donald Trump.

After a while, some of you had to turn away. You couldn't watch any longer. You couldn't stomach what you were seeing because you just couldn't believe this was happening. Not in America. Neither could I, even as I was battling insurrectionists and protecting our leaders.

I've been thinking about that day a lot. In terms of raw carnage, blood, guts, and destruction, you and I have seen much worse.

For decades we've viewed the bloodied, mauled, and maimed bodies of our American sons and daughters, chewed up by war, strewn across some faraway battlefield. Korea. Vietnam. Iran. The Persian Gulf. Somalia. Lebanon. Iraq. Afghanistan. We've seen the images of flag-covered coffins come home for heartbreaking ceremonies. The survivors with physical and mental injuries are daily reminders of their sacrifices.

We watched as our cities burned from the 1960s to the 1990s, torn apart by racial injustice and strife, and as hundreds of mostly Black people were shot and killed by police and the National Guard. Washington. New York. Chicago. Detroit. Newark. Memphis. Atlanta. Los Angeles. Baltimore. Houston. Miami. More than 120 cities alone erupted after Rev. Martin Luther King Jr. was assassinated in 1968.

Meanwhile, every year for the past twenty-two years, we have relived 9/11. We revisit that horrible footage of thousands of Americans who perished in the World Trade Center after our enemies crashed jetliners into the buildings. We watched people so helpless, so terrified, that they leaped from windows to certain death. We still weep for the first responders who perished trying to save them.

And then we saw the murder of George Floyd.

All of it was horrific, all of it unforgettable. But January 6th was different. This was a more vicious gut punch, one made even crueler because we didn't see it coming. The insurrectionists tried to destroy the very lifeblood of this nation, our democracy. This was not an attack on one piece of what we hold most dear, not one person, not one community, not one town, not one city. It was all our communities, all of us at the same time. It was everything we believe in.

And a lot of you cried. I cried too.

I cried that day when I was carrying a rioter who had been trampled by the mob to our medical unit for CPR. I was crying when I ran to Senator Mitch McConnell's side office door because we got a call that some of his staff had locked themselves in against the rioters and needed help.

Almost from birth, we are told that our country is special because we have a democracy. It is where every man and woman has a right—no, a duty—to have a say in how it operates.

"We, the people."

Those are the first three words of the US Constitution. We are told of its history and its founders—George Washington, Benjamin Franklin, Thomas Jefferson, James Madison, Alexander Hamilton, Nathan Hale, Patrick Henry. The American Revolution.

Yes, it was imperfect. Only white men who owned land could vote, and hundreds of thousands of people were excluded from the process because they were slaves. Still, we grew up proud that no kings or queens lorded over us. We have a "government of the people, by the people, for the people."

Our government has an even greater special significance for some of us. For African Americans, our belief in its promise has been almost like a religion. We needed to believe. We had to believe. We had no choice. This place wasn't right for us from the start. They brought us over in chains and changed our names and wiped out our culture even before there actually was an America.

But almost from its birth, we have been trying to get America to do what Martin Luther King said in 1963: "Rise up, live out the true meaning of its creed: We hold these truths to be self-evident that all men are created equal."

Our struggle for democracy has threaded through Crispus Attucks, the first person killed in the American Revolution; the trial before the Supreme Court for the men and women of the slave ship *La Amistad*; the Dred Scott and *Plessy v. Ferguson* decisions; the Civil War; the Thirteenth, Fourteenth, and Fifteenth Amendments; *Brown v. the Board of Education*; the civil rights movement; and service by African Americans in every American war, even when our country didn't want us there.

Immigrants felt a special pain that day too, whether they came to America more than one hundred years ago or just got here. America is the place on which they have pinned their hopes and dreams. Some fled tyranny and persecution in their home countries; others left grinding poverty, and many, religious or ethnic bigotry. When they searched for a better life, they were united in their belief in a place called America.

They quickly learned that our streets weren't paved with gold. Yes, there was discrimination here, but it was the government's job to protect them, not persecute them. They could fight that government and challenge that government to do what's right. They could vote, and their vote would matter. They could even be the government.

Consequently, immigrants, the children of immigrants, and the grandchildren of immigrants are interwoven in our government and our culture. No, America didn't always live up to its promise. We've had some horrible things happen here, like when the nation locked Japanese citizens in internment camps during World War II. Still, nobody is jumping on boats to flee America like they are doing all over the world. Why? Because it's America.

That's why January 6th hurt so much. It was a frightening wake-up call that our democracy, this thing we hold so precious, can be taken from us if we don't protect it. My fellow officers and I gave it our all on January 6th. We stood our ground, and because we did, our democracy is still standing. There are no tanks roaming our capital like in other nations after a coup. There is no martial law. There is no National Guard patrolling our streets.

And I still stand, and I continue to fight. It is why I testified, along with three fellow officers, before the January

6th Committee, so we can get to the bottom of what happened that day and what led up to it. It is why I testified in two trials of Oath Keepers, to make sure their leaders were convicted and sentenced to prison.

It is the same reason I have appeared on scores of news programs to talk about what happened. I don't do it because I want to be a celebrity. I do it because I want people to know what happened to me and to my fellow officers, and what almost happened to our nation.

Some people appreciate what I have to say. I have received thousands of letters thanking me and urging me to keep moving forward. I get praise daily through social media.

On the other hand, I have been vilified by folks like Tucker Carlson when he was at Fox News, Newsmax, and MAGA fans, people who would sacrifice our democracy in their worship of Trump. I have been cursed and called profane names, and my life has been threatened.

I've even been accused of doing what I do for the public attention. If there is one thing that I want you to know about me, it's this. I would give everything back, the Congressional Gold Medal, the meeting and medal from President Biden, every media interview, every television appearance, my trial testimony, and my appearance before a congressional committee, if it would mean that January 6th never happened. I don't give a damn about any of those things.

If January 6th hadn't happened, my fellow officers who lost their lives in the wake of that horrible day would be here to be loved by their families and friends and appreciated by other United States Capitol Police officers. If January 6th hadn't happened, I wouldn't have gone through the mental anguish that I did and that I am still working through with counseling. If January 6th hadn't happened, the place where I work wouldn't be filled with regret and bad memories around every corner. If January 6th hadn't happened, I wouldn't be the subject of lies and ridicule all over the internet.

I speak out not because I want something for me but because I want accountability. I want the people responsible for that day, including Trump and anybody else who conspired to breach the Capitol and try to halt our democracy, to pay a price, just like we paid a price. And I want us to never repeat a day like that. It is a stain on our nation.

And if my detractors think I can somehow be scared away with their bullshit accusations and threats, they don't know me. They don't know Harry Dunn.

I'll continue to use my voice to protect this country. I'll stand up to the lies and hate and racism and bigotry.

I will always be standing my ground to make sure our democracy exists. And I'll ask that you stand with me so that nothing like this ever happens again. We will get through this trauma. We will get through this nightmare, but only if we stand together.

1

PROTECTING
DEMOCRACY

Most people don't really know what we do as the Capitol Police. Before January 6th, many Americans probably didn't know we existed, and many still don't truly understand what we do, including my new friend Michael Fanone. Mike is the former Washington, DC, police officer who was seriously injured on January 6th while fighting alongside me and other officers to protect the Capitol. He joined the Capitol Police in the wake of the terrorist attacks on September 11, 2001, because that's the kind of guy he is. He stayed in the role for a few years before becoming a DC police officer.

At some point after January 6th, Mike erroneously said Capitol Police were "glorified security guards." Nothing could be further from the truth. The department didn't suit Mike because he wanted the adrenaline rush of being a street cop—undercover drug busts, dramatic take-downs, and car chases with squealing tires.

We can do that too, but that's not what we tend to do.

In early 2023, for example, we were closing in on a car reported stolen not far from the Capitol and across the street from where members of Congress frequently hold television interviews. Two guys bolted from the car. We caught one right away. The other escaped into an apartment building and barricaded himself in a third-floor unit. We contained the area and brought out our negotiations team.

Ultimately, we dispatched the SWAT unit. The SWAT unit was literally seconds from breaching the door of the apartment when the second suspect surrendered after a seven-hour standoff. Inside the car, we found a 9 mm handgun that had been turned into a machine-gun pistol and an M-4 rifle, like the one I carry at the Capitol. The rifle was a "ghost gun," which means the parts were purchased online and put together without the rifle being registered.

I am certified in M-4 weaponry and carry my registered rifle while I'm on duty to protect people in- and outside the Capitol. The weapons those guys had, however, are for committing crime. They can't be connected to an individual if they are recovered by law enforcement.

So, like I said, we have the capacity for that intense degree of law enforcement, and more, but that's not our day-to-day.

The Capitol Police have lots of capabilities, in part because we are a relatively large police department. No, we're not New York or Los Angeles or Chicago or even Atlanta, but, according to the Justice Department, our two thousand officers make us a far larger force than 90 percent of the nation's more than 12,200 local police departments and three thousand sheriff's offices. Plus, we have all the machinery of most big-city departments—in some cases, even more.

The Capitol Police have motorcycle cops, cops in cars, and a canine unit. We have a Riot Control Unit with all the special gear that big-city departments have. We have a Hazardous Devices Section, a Hazardous Material Response Team, Special Operations, and a Crime Scene Search Team. We have a Containment and Emergency Response Unit and a SWAT team. We have a Crisis Negotiation Unit, Reports Processing Team, Court Liaison Unit, and Special Events Section. I could go on, but I think you get the point.

As a visitor to the Capitol, you seldom see members of those units. If you do, you've crossed into a bad space. The most visible element of the department is the Uniformed Services Bureau. That's guys like me. We are a 24/7 team of officers who provide security for the Capitol and congressional office buildings. Our protection area goes from as far as H Street on the north side, P Street on the south side, Seventh Street on the east side, and Third Street on the west side. It is divided into the Capitol Division, which, obviously, is assigned to the entire Capitol, as well as a unit assigned to the House of Representatives, another to the US Senate, and another that covers the Library of Congress.

We provide security and protection to the members and staff at three Senate office buildings that run along Constitution Avenue north of the Capitol: the Russell Senate Office Building, the Dirksen Senate Office Building, and the Hart Senate Office Building. We are also responsible for three buildings on Independence Avenue south of the Capitol: Cannon House Office Building, the Longworth House Office Building, and the Rayburn House Office Building.

These buildings house the members of the House of Representatives and their staff. To the untrained eye, a lot of what we do could appear to be the work of security guards. We screen visitors to the Capitol Complex. We tamp down crime in and around the Capitol. We enhance relations with the community and its citizens as we help people find their way around a sprawling complex.

What my friend Mike didn't understand is that while we do all the things other police departments do, our core mission is not to fight crime. Our mission is to protect, to prevent crime, and to provide a safe space for democracy to function. Our job is not to chase a crime after it happens, which is the primary function of most police departments. Our job is to keep it from happening. Think about it for a moment. Do you think people—foreign and domestic—haven't tried to shut down the Capitol and hold the nation hostage before January 6th? Do you think people with a grudge against a member of Congress or a senator haven't wanted to take one of them out?

No?

In October 1983, an Israeli visiting the United States entered the Capitol with two plastic bottles filled with a flammable liquid, gunpowder, and improvised shrapnel. The device was rigged to a detonator with copper wire. He planned to explode it where it could do the most damage. Four plainclothes Capitol Police officers stopped him before he could. A month later, in a bathroom in the Capitol, two American members of a communist organization assembled a bomb that detonated and caused extensive damage. Fortunately, no one was killed or injured. After an investigation, they were tried and imprisoned.

In 1998, a man with a history of paranoid schizophrenia, which included being committed for nearly two months in a Montana hospital, triggered the metal detector at a Capitol entrance. He was carrying a gun. When Capitol Police approached him, he shot and killed one officer and then wounded a tourist and another officer. He ran into the office of a member of Congress and fatally shot a Capitol Police detective who was assigned to protect the member of Congress. Before dying, the detective shot the man four times. The gunman survived and was subdued and arrested by two other police officers. Several lives were saved by that Capitol Police detective.

There are other examples, including the anthrax letters a terrorist sent to two senators in the Capitol following the 9/11 attacks on the World Trade Center and the Pentagon. Those, though, should be enough to help you understand that our job is to ensure that the women and men you send to Washington to do your business have a safe place to do it, regardless of their party affiliation or politics. Yes, what they do is messy, it is complicated, and it is noisy. At times, it can be exasperating and tiresome. Still, it is the government we have chosen. So, we protect them.

We also make sure that when you or your church, mosque, synagogue, or other organization comes to the Capitol to have your voice heard, you are protected, whether you come individually or in the tens or the hundreds or the thousands. You see us perform our job day after day, year after year. It's all so baked into our democracy that you hardly think about it. Let me give you two quick examples of what I'm talking about.

In early 2023, Republicans bargained and shouted and called each other names while they voted fifteen times over several days to decide whether Congressman

Kevin McCarthy of California would be the new Speaker of the House of Representatives. While they did, no elected representatives could be sworn in as members of the 118th Congress. So, the House couldn't get to work. The media, some Democrats, and late-night talk-show comedians made fun of them. But that was our democracy at work, going about its business, doing what it does.

Now, here is where the Capitol Police come in. Congressional Republicans could hold that vote on January 7, 2023, because we provided a place for them to hash out their differences that was safe from protesters, extremists, and anyone else who would try to halt the process. Ironically, if Capitol Police officers had not shed blood to protect many of those same legislators from a rampaging mob at the Capitol on almost exactly the same date two years earlier, they may not have been able to cast those votes when they did.

And many of the people in that room, squabbling over whether McCarthy should be the Speaker, were some of the same 137 Republican members who voted to overturn the 2020 election two years earlier, even after we had put our lives on the line to protect it and them. But that's our job, regardless of party or politics.

In September 2009, I was working my first huge demonstration. Barack Obama was the president. I had just been sworn in. I was probably only weeks out of training. It was a normal autumn day, cool and cloudy, but there was a sea of people outside the Capitol. There must have been seventy thousand demonstrators. They filled up the west lawn and spilled out onto the National Mall.

The demonstration was called the Tea Party Express. The Tea Party was a conservative movement within the Republican Party that started right after Obama's first presidential inauguration. That day, people came from all over the country. I remember looking at the crowd and thinking, "If these people decided to go into the Capitol, there's no way we could stop them."

The event began as a demonstration against the Affordable Care Act, which, by now, everyone was calling Obamacare. But it morphed into a demonstration against anything Obama. Some people were hollering about gun rights and singing "God Bless America," but mostly they were protesting and cursing Obama. Some of them were chanting, "Liar! Liar! Liar! Liar!" because that was what Rep. Joe Wilson, a Republican from South Carolina, had called Obama three days earlier during his first State of the Union address. One person had a sign that called Obama the "parasite in chief." Other people had signs that basically said he was a Black Adolf Hitler.

In the crowd, one guy had a sign supporting Obamacare. The other people in the crowd didn't like that, and they began calling him names. They cursed him and basically called him a bum.

"Go get a job, you asshole," one of them shouted.

"You just want the government to take care of you," another said. "Get a fucking job."

The guy stood his ground and shouted back, "I've got a job. I go to work every day, but I can't get enough hours on my job to have health insurance."

I kept my eyes on that guy to make sure he could protest without being attacked by other people in the group. They were loud and nasty, but they weren't a physical threat. That was my first real hint of what the Capitol Police's core function is. Like I said earlier, our job is to provide a safe place for democracy to take place. My job that day was to protect the Americans who came to Washington and wanted to curse the president and call the Congress names. At the same time, I needed to make sure that guy on the other side of the debate could have his opinion heard too.

I didn't truly understand the depth of everything that was going on. I was young, just a few years out of college. But I was watching part of democracy at work. This wasn't some shit you read about in a history book. This wasn't a theory about how things are supposed to work. It was happening in the now, right in front of my eyes. This was democracy in action. These were real people being crazy passionate about what they believed in, whether I liked it or not, whether I agreed with them or not, whether anybody inside the Capitol agreed with them or not.

I didn't see a Black face in that crowd. A lot of the people there that day probably weren't terribly fond of my Black ass, but it didn't matter. They were Americans, executing their rights as Americans. Unless someone committed a real crime, no one would be arrested, tried, executed, shot, or disappeared. They would make their voices heard and then return safely to their homes, where they could continue to exercise their right by voting out the people they didn't like. In how many other countries could they do that without paying a cost? And I was a vital part of making that happen. On that day, the importance of our institutions, our rights, and my place in it hadn't completely sunk in. To me, it was still just a job. It would take a few more years before protecting democracy became a part of the very fiber of my being, something I would give my life for. On January 6th, I almost did.

The truth is, I never wanted to be a police officer, not for the Capitol, not for the city, not for anybody. I didn't have anything against cops. I just never wanted to be one. Well, I can't say never ever. When you're in elementary school, they ask you what you want to be, and they put up pictures of a firefighter, a police officer, a nurse, a doctor, a teacher, or some other bullshit that society had pretty much programmed you to say. You pick one of the above.

A police officer was always made out to be one of the most desirable, and certainly one of the most honorable. They never asked if you wanted to be a Wall Street investment banker making millions of dollars or a restaurant owner or the inventor of the next great zillion-dollar thing that would revolutionize the world. Hell, they could have suggested owning a chain of McDonald's restaurants. Everybody loved McDonald's. That would have been a very admirable goal.

That said, by the time I reached junior high school, being a police officer certainly wasn't my dream. I would say that's probably true for at least half the people I know who have become police officers. It was not their dream job. Like me, they stumbled into it, or they were recruited into it. Some might have come from a family of police officers, which led them into the profession. You know, granddad was a police officer, dad was a police officer, their uncle was a police officer, their cousin was a police officer. I hear that happens a lot in cities like Boston or Philadelphia or areas of Long Island, New York, or Staten Island in New York City, where whole neighborhoods became New York City cops.

In some cases, they came from a military background. In some cases, being a cop seemed the natural thing to do. In fact, some of the guys I've talked with over the years went into the military with the idea of landing a job in law enforcement because they believed their military experience would give them an advantage. Police officer. Border Patrol. State Highway Patrol. And that was true for a long time, back in the days when being a cop meant kicking ass and taking names. These days though, some departments are beginning to rethink that philosophy because being a cop, at least being a good cop, has very little to do with what they train you to do in the military.

I was never in the military, but my dad was. He served in the US Air Force. In the military, you're trained to follow orders and accomplish the mission, which is also true with the police. But in the military, you're trained to overpower and kill the enemy. Yes, there are other skills you learn in the process, but that is the purpose of the military. Seldom do you interact with civilians.

In policing, interacting with civilians is 90 percent of the job, and American citizens are not the enemy, though some police officers treat some of them that way. They are the people we are paid to protect from the bad guys and sometimes from themselves. We also serve in a lot of ways, from pointing residents to counseling for their knuckleheaded teenage son or belligerent daughter to attending the neighborhood-watch meeting to talk with community members about crime trends in their neighborhood to directing traffic, helping everyone get from one place to the next.

In our line of work, even the bad guys are not necessarily the "enemy." Many people will have one, two, maybe even three real brushes with the law. I'm not talking about traffic tickets but shoplifting, drug possession arrests, and even first-time felonies. Yes, they have committed crimes, but they should not be branded as criminals.

Criminals are the handful of Americans who have made a conscious decision that preying on other people will be their profession, their way of life. No, they don't want a job. They don't want to start a legitimate business. They have decided to abuse other people to get rich. I'm talking about everybody from serious drug traffickers and professional robbers to people like Bernie Madoff, who stole billions from hardworking Americans in a Ponzi scheme, to the people who ripped off billions in taxpayer money from Paycheck Protection Plan loans during the pandemic.

So, being a police officer, whether on my side of the street or in Mike's job with the DC Police Department, is a much more nuanced profession. You wade through a lot of factors when you're doing your job.

For Black people, the idea of becoming a cop has a few more wrinkles. A lot of Black people became cops because they wanted to change what they saw as a corrupt and abusive system. In their neighborhoods, the police were not their friends. In poorer Black communities, by and large, the police were a vulgar, oppressive force. They rode herd over Black people. They treated you like shit. They talked to you like shit. It didn't matter who you were—moms, dads, sisters, brothers, children. It didn't matter. So, some Black folks believed they could change police departments from the inside.

We never had problems with the police in my neighborhood. Clinton, Maryland, where I grew up, is a small, predominately Black suburb about twenty miles southeast of Washington, DC. My community was single-family homes and very working class. There was no crime, no robberies or break-ins, no drug dealers, no gangs. Kids played on the streets and in the parks. It was a carefree existence. I lived with my mom and dad and two of my four sisters. Back then, we just made up play. When you went outside, you looked for where the bicycles were stacked up in somebody's yard or on a corner.

"That's Mike's bike. That's Eric's bike."

You found your friends, and you just jumped in with whatever everybody was doing. You might be playing basketball in someone's backyard, or there was this wooded area where we played. You really didn't see police officers. If you saw them, they were polite and respected. So, it was cool.

Another incentive for Black people to get a job with the police, particularly for those of us who grew up around the federal government in DC or in big cities, was that government jobs meant long-term stability. In most of the nation's urban centers, jobs like police officer and firefighter come with incredible stability, which includes insurance and great pensions.

Police and firefighters always had unions, and they negotiated great retirement packages. You do your twenty or thirty years and you can retire relatively young with a great income for the rest of your life, sometimes as much as 85 percent of your final salary. So, that's a big incentive, particularly for a young Black man in a country where having a career—not a job but a career—has seldom been held out as an attainable goal.

That said, I still didn't want to be a police officer.

2

GROWING INTO
THE JOB

By the end of high school, I had my eyes set on becoming a professional athlete. I know what you're thinking: too many kids, especially Black kids, have their hopes fixed on professional sports. It's the focus of sweat-filled dreams—the NFL, NBA, or MLB. Yes, I had those dreams too, and I know the odds. But I had a lot going for me. I had great parents who stood with me and made it possible for me to have everything I needed to succeed in junior high and high school sports. I had a great work ethic that I learned from my dad. I had size and, thanks to some great coaches in college, I developed my skills. I got close, tantalizingly close. Maybe if I had been more patient, I could have had that professional career.

I began my growth spurt in junior high. I grew to six feet two by the eighth grade. By high school, I was six feet five. It was to be expected. My dad is six feet five, and my mom is five feet nine. By my senior year, I weighed 275 pounds. So, I was big. I was deep into sports. I was the starting center for the Surrattsville High School Hornets. I didn't score a lot, but I led Prince George's County in rebounds and blocks in my senior year. It's been a while, but I think I averaged about ten points and thirteen rebounds a game. We went to the playoffs every year, but we weren't good enough for a championship.

I also played offensive tackle on the football team. We sucked as a football team. We had a good running back who ended up at Purdue University, but we didn't have anything else. I did well, mostly because I was big for a high school player. I didn't really have any skills. I was just bigger than everybody, so I could push people around, kind of like the portrayal of Michael Oher in the movie *The Blind Side*. The year I graduated, I was voted all–Prince George's County in football and basketball. I was proud of my accomplishments, but it was on to the next step. Fortunately for me, I had basketball and football scholarship offers. I felt I needed to decide which to pursue.

Basketball was really my first love, but I knew I didn't have the speed and skills to compete in the NBA. I was big for high school, but I was undersized for the pros. I'd have to play guard or small forward, and I didn't have the required speed or dribbling skills. I saw a better chance to go to the NFL than the NBA, so football won out.

I had several scholarship opportunities. So, my parents and I began what I thought would be several "official visits" to colleges and universities. James Madison University in Harrisonburg, Virginia, was the first stop. It was also the last. I accepted their offer without setting foot on campus. I know what you're thinking. I should have visited more schools, but I didn't understand the process. My parents didn't understand the process. My high school coaches didn't understand.

I did it because it was the first offer I had, but I have never regretted it. I knew that was where I wanted to be from the moment I arrived at the campus. There was just something about it. It's only two hours from Clinton, but the way it's tucked away up in the mountains, it felt like I was in another place. It's not something I can really put my finger on, but from the moment I got there, I felt like I belonged. It felt like a community, like a family.

Plus, I had a ball while I was there.

The football players showed me around the campus. It's really a pretty place. Even though the school has about twenty thousand students, it didn't feel big. The first night, we went to a basketball game. After the game, we went to house parties with the upperclassmen, so I could experience party life. I was young and dumb. What my social life might be was important to me and, at that point, more important than academics. We went to three or four parties that night. There were girls everywhere.

There was not a lot of dancing. People were talking and drinking while the music was playing.

The girls were fresh, ready to have a good time, flirty as hell, but no, nothing happened. The next day, we went to a ski resort not far from the school. I went tubing in the snow. That was a first. The thing I liked about JMU then, and that I found to be true throughout my years there, is that it felt like everybody cared about each other. The Purple and Gold. You went to a party at someone's place, and they treated you like you were friends, even if they didn't know you.

"Come on in. Grab a beer. Make yourself at home."

There was a lot of love. People supported each other. After I left, I still maintained strong ties with people from the university community, and when I testified before the January 6th Committee, the JMU community supported me through their web pages and on social media. They stand by me and what I'm doing, and that's a good feeling.

In my first year at James Madison, I was redshirted, which meant I was on the team, but I wasn't going to play in my freshman year. Redshirting was a common practice in college athletics at the time. The coach might feel a certain freshman wasn't ready to start or couldn't move up the chart in front of the guys already playing the position. Redshirting allowed that player to retain four years of eligibility to play if they attended college for longer than the typical four years. Even Herschel Walker, one of the greatest running backs in the history of college football, and running back Marshall Faulk, who is now in the NFL Hall of Fame, were redshirted in their freshman year. I had a year to work on myself. I had to get stronger, get bigger, get faster. One of the things you learn quickly when you get to the college football level is that everyone is big, and everyone is fast, and everyone comes with a great athletic résumé.

The first thing our head coach did was sit all the freshmen down as a group and, in essence, tell us that we weren't shit. His name was Mickey Matthews. If you thought you were special, he had ridded you of that idea by the time he finished talking to you.

"Stand up if you were selected all-state," Coach Matthews said.

A few players stood up.

"Stand up if you were chosen all-county," he said.

More of us, including me, stood up.

"Stand up if you were all-city."

A few more players stood up.

"Stand up if you were the captain of the football team."

By the time he finished, we were all standing up.

"All that shit you did in high school doesn't mean shit in here," Coach said. "You're now with the best of the best."

After that talk, I knew I had to get better fast, or I was done. We had players from all over. A lot of them were from all across the Tidewater region: Hampton, Norfolk, Newport News, Virginia Beach. We also had a bunch of guys out of Georgia. My line coach, Coach Zernhelt, was frustrated with me when we started out because, like I said, I didn't have any skills. I was uncoordinated. The first thing I had to work on was perfecting my stance. People smaller than me knocked me on my ass because they had better technique than I did.

Coach Z, that's what we called him, stayed on my ass.

"Harry, when you're in your stance, put your weight on your quads," Coach Z said.

"Coach, that hurts," I said.

"That's because your quads are not strong enough. You have to strengthen your quads."

"Harry, lead with your left foot."

"Harry, when you hit somebody, you want to hit them on your second step."

"Harry, when you hit a guy, deliver that blow with your foot on the ground. Otherwise, you don't have leverage."

I played behind a guy named Kevin Mapp. Kevin was good, really good. He was one or two years older than me. That's why they redshirted me in my first year. There was no way I was going to beat out him or any of the backups. In the second game of my sophomore year, Kevin tore his Achilles tendon right before halftime. We were playing Hofstra in New York. I had had a great week of practice. The coach said, "Harry, you're in."

The first play we ran a trap, and I pulled. I was the lead blocker. Suddenly, this linebacker hit me and I went airborne. *Bam!* He rocked me. My whole body hurt. I thought, "Is this what the rest of my career is going to be like?" We won the game, but by the time it was over I knew I had to get better. A lot better.

The torn Achilles ended Kevin's playing career at JMU. By the next year, I was a beast. I was close to 330 pounds, and it was all muscle. I had worked so damn hard. There were winter workouts. During spring break, you got spring practice. In the summer, you went home for a week and then you were doing summer workout. You took classes in the summer, and you worked out. The next season, it showed. The people who stayed were the better performers on the team.

When training camp came around in August, you were running circles around the other players because they were trying to get in shape and you were already there.

I started the rest of the 2002 season and all of the 2003 season. I loved being a lineman. We were the biggest, toughest, strongest guys on the team, and we were essential. The quarterback couldn't be good without us giving him the time to throw. The running back couldn't be good without us creating holes for him to run through. We do the work, but we don't get the credit. As our offensive line coach told us, if we don't give them time, none of this shit works.

My 2004 season started well, but I hurt my shoulder, and I couldn't continue as one of the starting tackles. I contributed, but I was hampered by the injury. So, I was substituted into a lot of games. But it didn't matter, because that was a great year for our team. We won the 1-AA National Championship. James Madison had never won one. That's just to let you know, it was a big deal. (JMU won a second championship in 2016.)

But in 2004, we were phenomenal. We went 13–2. We were the first and only team to win three games on the road to advance to the National Championship game. Linemen, like me, were crucial to our success. We were definitely a running team. In the championship game, we ran for 314 yards and passed for only 132. After we were crowned national champions, you couldn't tell me a damn thing. We were the champions. Couldn't anybody tell us shit. Nope. No humility. We had these big championship rings. We wore them everywhere. I wore mine for years.

My last year, in 2005, was a good year. We didn't go back to the championship game, but we averaged 404 yards of total offense a game, and 235 of that was the run game. I got invitations for tryouts to several NFL teams: the Washington Redskins, the Buffalo Bills, the Pittsburgh Steelers, the Jacksonville Jaguars, the Indianapolis Colts, the Carolina Panthers, and one or two more I can't remember. Unfortunately, none of them panned out.

I tried out for and was signed by the Montreal Alouettes in the Canadian Football League. Lots of NFL
players started in the CFL before crossing over to the
NFL. In college, quarterback Joe Theismann played with
Notre Dame and then played three seasons in the CFL
with the Toronto Argonauts before going to Washington
in the NFL, where he took the team to two Super Bowls,
beating the Miami Dolphins in one and losing to the
Raiders in the other. Unfortunately, his career ended on
national television in a *Monday Night Football* game, when
all-everything New York Giants linebacker Lawrence
Taylor broke Theismann's leg on a devastating hit.

Jeff Garcia was a backup quarterback with the Calgary
Stampeders until his fifth and final CFL season. That
year, he led Calgary to the Grey Cup title, the CFL's
equivalent of our Super Bowl. Garcia then signed with
the San Francisco 49ers in the NFL as the backup to
future Hall of Fame quarterback Steve Young. After
Young's career ended because of a devastating hit in a
game, Garcia became the starter. He was selected for the
Pro Bowl three times in his five seasons with San
Francisco.

Center Brett Jones played for the Calgary Stampeders
and was very successful before going to the New York
Giants, and Warren Moon, one of the NFL's greatest
quarterbacks, started his career with the Edmonton Eski-
mos before signing on with what was then the Houston

Oilers. Moon was so successful that he is the only player to be inducted into the NFL Pro Football Hall of Fame and the CFL Hall of Fame.

So, playing with the Alouettes seemed a logical step to getting to the NFL. Many athletes, including a defensive back on my JMU team who signed with the Alouettes the same year I did, played their whole careers in the CFL. It's a good living, and you're doing the thing you love to do. Anyway, I had a great training camp with the team that year. I played twice in preseason games against the Winnipeg Blue Bombers. The line coach said, "Harry, you are killing it."

But then I was hospitalized for a damned foot infection. It was bad—so bad that I had to stay in the hospital for two days. I couldn't play that year, so I was cut. It wasn't a great feeling, but I still had hopes. I wasn't cut because I wasn't good enough. I was good, but I caught a bad break. I headed back to Clinton. I worked in clubs as a bouncer and busted my ass to stay in shape for another shot at football. I played a lot of basketball, and it actually surprised me how good I was. I was playing against college kids and former NBA players.

The next year, Montreal asked me to try out for the team again. I had another great camp, even better than the previous year. I was kicking ass. I was getting all this praise from my coaches. But then I was summoned to the general manager's office, and they told me to bring my playbook. I knew what that meant. I was being cut. I said to myself, "This has gotta be a joke. I'm balling." But I headed to the general manager's office.

"Hey man, we got to let you go," the general manager said.

He's not giving me much. He's not explaining anything, offering me anything.

I said, "No, you've got the wrong dude. I belong here."

All he said was, "After lunch, you turn in your playbook and wait for your flight home."

I didn't get it. I truly didn't understand. I was playing well. It was a hard reality to accept, but I had to. I began preparations to head home. While I was packing, I got a call from the line coach.

"Harry, where the hell are you?" he asked. "We're meeting. Get your ass down here."

"Coach," I said. "I'm heading home. I've been cut. I turned in my playbook."

The coach was just as confused as I was.

"No way," he said. "Don't go anywhere until you hear from me. Let me talk to some people and just come to the meeting room."

When he showed up, he was furious. Unfortunately, even he couldn't fix what was wrong.

"Harry, you're doing great," he said. "You are having a great camp, and you belong here. This has nothing to do with your play. This is business. We've got too many

Americans on the team. You're better than the other guy, but he's Canadian."

I was hurt. I was good enough, even better than good, but the CFL had its rules. A certain percentage of the team had to be Canadian nationals, and only a certain number of starters could be American. I was assed out. When I returned to Clinton this time, I was angry. I was angry and hurt. I'm good enough. I know it. They know it. But I can't get a job because of some rules that have nothing to do with my abilities. "Fuck it! Fuck this politics shit!"

To be honest, I hadn't completely given up on playing professional football. I loved the game. I loved demolishing people on the line. I loved the feeling when me and another lineman double-team blocked a guy and put him on his ass. Afterward, we would dap each other up. "Yeah, we crushed that motherfucker." But for now, that would have to wait. I was back in the DC area, and I needed to work. I landed a job with Enterprise Rent-A-Car. They liked hiring college athletes because we had a sense of teamwork, which was really important in their operation. They even based a major television commercial campaign on that philosophy.

It was a cool gig. I met lots of different types of people. I've always been a curious, talkative person, so it worked well for me. Plus, I'm so big that I stand out. People are attracted to me because of my size, and I'm attracted to them because I'm curious. I was working the counter one day, and this lady walked in, and we got to talking. She was a Capitol Police officer. She told me a little about the job and urged me to apply. She told me they would have a booth at a career fair at Martin's Crosswinds. Martin's Crosswinds is this huge ballroom facility in Greenbelt, Maryland, where people in the DC area have all kinds of events, weddings, retirements, balls. Then she said the magic words: "And we get paid really well."

I went to the career fair and talked to the Capitol Police. They told me the salary, and I said, "They pay how much?!" The starting salary back then was $65,000. I was twenty-three or twenty-four years old. And they said you could work overtime and double that. I'm thinking, "Man, if I work overtime, I can make $100,000 in a year. Sign me up!"

It took me a long time to get hired, almost a year. You have to do the physical and a polygraph exam and then they bring you in for a background check. There's a psychological check and a vision and hearing examination. Then I went through a long interview process. They checked out all my references. There was more waiting. Finally, I was accepted and learned I would be reporting to the Federal Law Enforcement Training Center in Glynco, Georgia.

Glynco is really a town created by the government. In 1942, during World War II, the government put a naval air station on the land and called it Glynco. The name was created by pushing together two parts of its location, Glynn County. When it was no longer needed as an air station, around 1974, the government turned it into the Federal Law Enforcement Training Center. Everybody refers to it as FLETC (pronounced flet-see). The center is a town unto itself with its own zip code. It's located just northwest of Brunswick, Georgia, which is also in Glynn County. Brunswick, as you may recall, is where an unarmed Black man, Ahmaud Arbery, was out for a morning run when he was gunned down by three white men who thought he looked suspicious.

FLETC is where all the federal law enforcement people train before they branch off into their own service: the Bureau of Alcohol, Tobacco, Firearms, and Explosives; Border Patrol; Secret Service; FBI; and the rest. My class of Capitol Police officers did three months of training there before we returned to Maryland for three more months of training. Not long after I was hired by the Capitol Police, the Montreal Alouettes called my agent and invited me up again. I was making preparations to head to FLETC. Maybe the third time with Montreal would be the charm, but I was madly in love with a woman, and I had a chance at a career. I was ready to move on from football, and I turned them down.

I don't know what I was expecting, but FLETC is a huge facility. It stretches out across 1,600 acres. It has classrooms, dormitories, and a dining hall that can serve more than four thousand meals per day. It has eighteen firearms ranges, including an indoor range complex with 146 separate firing points. In addition to that, it has eight semi-enclosed ranges with two hundred places from which to shoot. Then, they've got this complex of driver training courses, where they teach you how to do high-speed chases and how to handle yourself and your car, like using it for protection when you pull up on an incident. As part of the training, they made us lose control of the car and then figure out how to get control back.

They built a whole fake neighborhood with thirty-four houses and other buildings that were equipped with video cameras to record our actions during point-of-entry exercises or room-to-room searches. We could watch the video later to learn how to fine-tune what we were doing. It was deep. They had interviewing suites where we learned how to interrogate suspects. That's where we got to use what is called "verbal judo." It's like martial arts applied to talking with people. There were mock court-rooms, computer forensics laboratories, and other laboratories for fingerprinting and identifying narcotics.

I carpooled to Glynco with a guy, Richardson Philius. I didn't know anybody else there. We stayed in a hotel when we first got there. Usually you stay in a dormitory, but the base was crowded, and it has a partnership with hotels. We were only five minutes away from the center.

We would be in the center until we were finished for the day. Class normally ended at 4 p.m. They started with roll call at 7 a.m. The Capitol Police officers trained as a unit. There were about forty of us. It was eight hours a day—marksmanship, driving techniques, police tactics, situational awareness. One of the biggest things they drilled us on was the law. There was a lot of that, over and over again, and there was a lot to learn.

We did a ton of running and conditioning. It definitely got us into shape. It was a different shape than football. That was a huge adjustment for me. We went on runs for two or three miles every day. As a football player, as a lineman, I only had to be fast over a short distance, maybe ten to twenty yards. So, those three-mile runs were a struggle. The bad thing was that I was one of the squad leaders. As a squad leader, I was supposed to be at the front of the squad. On those long runs, somebody else had to be in the front.

After three months in Glynco, our class moved north to train for another three months at a different FLETC, this one in Cheltenham, Maryland. It's about fifteen miles from downtown Washington, not far from where I grew up. They train lots of people from more than seventy-five agencies in the area. Our training still included running and conditioning and staying in shape, and they had firing ranges so we could keep up our marksmanship.

But I guess more than anything, we were learning local law. We knew federal law, but we were operating in the District of Columbia, and we had to learn how laws applied in the district versus how they applied federally. For instance, federally, marijuana is illegal, but in DC it's not. What about the use of deadly force? Federal law says if they are running away, you may be covered when shooting at a felon. But your department may have a policy that says you can't do that. Federally, you can fire a warning shot, but Capitol Police regulations say no warning shot.

By then I had changed. I was obviously in better shape. I had learned all these driving and shooting skills, and I was certainly schooled in federal law. But I also noticed that I was more aware of my surroundings. When I entered a room, I immediately looked around for the exits. I noticed which way a door opened and closed, outward or inward. I looked at the elevator buttons differently because I now knew that the star button would take me to the nearest exit. I saw the world differently. I was more vigilant. I didn't automatically see a person as a bad guy, but I made up scenarios in my head. What if somebody pops out of that door and starts shooting? What is my plan of escape, or how would I attack him? How would I get people out in an emergency?

I graduated with my class in June 2009, class 161. The graduation took place in the Russell Senate Office

Building. There were about forty other officers. My wife, Danyel, was there. We got married just days earlier, on May 22, 2009. My parents, Harry and Joyce Dunn, were there. I don't remember much about that day. At the time, it just felt like another day. Nothing too significant. But I do remember that I graduated on a Friday and started at the Capitol the following Monday.

I've touched on this, but I quickly learned that one of my main jobs at the Capitol is to protect your right to free speech. The public sees the huge historic demonstrations that occur at the Capitol, but we also have lots of smaller demonstrations. There seems to be something going on almost daily. In my time here, we have had people come to the Capitol and just read the Bible twenty-four hours a day for a week, which I've learned is the maximum length of time for a legal demonstration. We've had demonstrations for DC statehood, people protesting genocide and oppression in other countries, a protest to ban infant circumcision, a real-life Nazi passing out Nazi propaganda to people walking around the building, minimum wage protests, protests to raise taxes, protests to lower taxes, protests for Obamacare, protests against Obamacare, protests against Scientology. It's surprising sometimes what gets people going.

Recently, I saw two women walking around with a sign that read, "Thank You for Everything, Capitol Police." That felt nice. We are starting to see more of that.

Anybody can protest, but there are rules for demonstrations that need to be followed if you don't want to get arrested or have your stuff torn down. All of it is explained in the application that everybody has to fill out in order to get permission for organized demonstrations. For instance, there are designated areas around the Capitol where people can protest. There's a map on the government website that shows where those areas are. And you can't protest inside the Capitol under any circumstances. Another rule: when demonstrators use loudspeakers, they have to be pointed away from the building.

Demonstrators can have all the flags or props they want, but they have to be freestanding. There are lots of things you can't do. For instance, you can't offer anything for sale, you can't ask for contributions, and you can't advertise. Also, you can't have any form of shelter, camping equipment, tents, sleeping bags, or bedrolls.

I learned after being on the job that some demonstrators want to get arrested because they want to emphasize the importance of their issue. We get tipped off in some cases, because it says on the application how many people they have and that they plan to get arrested. In those cases, it's easy for us, because we make preparations to arrest them and take them to jail. In other cases, in that space on the application, we get a note that says "intentions unknown." Those can be a little worrisome because you don't know what's going to happen. Somebody could get out of hand, and we would have to respond.

Some people come to the Capitol and just push the boundaries. We had one guy, Rivas Grogan, who would come and stand outside the Capitol and shout all day. His issue was abortion. He said this one thing over and over: "Abortion is the murdering of little babies! Save the babies!"

And he's shouting as loud as he can. I can hear it even now. He did it so much, it just stayed in my brain. He would shout that from everywhere around the Capitol. He was on the House side. He was on the Senate side, day after day after day. He was shouting so loud and so much that he brought lemons and bottles of honey with him and mixed them together in a tonic to soothe his throat so he could shout some more.

I guess the tonic helped, because he would be there all day, shouting at the Capitol, exercising his First Amendment right. It was irritating, but that was his constitutional right. Freedom of speech. But for some reason, Rivas started to push it too far. One day some members of Congress were outside the Capitol giving a press conference. I have no idea what they were talking about. They do this all the time, and, when they do, we have to police off the area. Rivas was out there, screaming and yelling. No matter how annoying, it is the right of an individual. All of a sudden, he sprinted toward the podium where the Congress people were speaking. I mean he was flat-out running in a threatening manner. Capitol Police officer Ty Bond and I took off after him and intercepted him before he got to the podium. We put him in handcuffs and led him away before anything could happen.

I don't know what was happening with Rivas, but not long after that, in October 2012, he was arrested after he ran onto the field during a National League Division Series playoff game between the Cincinnati Reds and the San Francisco Giants. He was holding a sign. On one side it read "antiabortion." On the other side was a photograph of Mitt Romney, who he was endorsing for the presidency against then President Barack Obama.

We arrested him again a few months later during Obama's second inauguration. Rivas climbed forty feet up a tree, where he wasn't allowed to be, and started shouting and hollering during the ceremony. He had already been arrested for demonstrating inside the Supreme Court. Rivas was from Los Angeles. The judge banned him from coming to DC until it was time for him to stand trial on misdemeanor charges.

As I said, as officers, we act without allegiance to party or politics. For instance, we arrested a guy named Manuel Oliver in March 2023 after he disrupted a congressional hearing, particularly when Republican congressman Pat Fallon of Texas, with whom he disagreed, was speaking. Oliver's son Joaquin was seventeen when he was killed on Valentine's Day five years earlier in the mass shooting at Marjory Stoneman Douglas High School in Parkland, Florida. Joaquin was one of seventeen people murdered in the shooting; another seventeen were injured. Fortunately for Oliver, he received a citation arrest, which means he wasn't taken to jail, but he was wrestled to the ground and handcuffed. Do I feel for Oliver and his wife, Patricia? Sure, I do. Do I think we need to do more to control gun violence? Most definitely. Still, democracy, no matter which side you are on, must be allowed to proceed.

In the beginning, being a Capitol Police officer was just a job to me. I mean, it was a good job. It paid well. It was an important job. It was a challenging job. But it was just a job. I was just trying to learn the ropes. I was more concerned about the logistics, learning where I was going to park my truck, and trying to understand what my supervisors wanted from me. When we had those large demonstrations, my attitude was, "Take y'all asses home. I want to play PlayStation. I want to go to the gym." I was starstruck too. The first time I saw Nancy Pelosi and some of the other Congress people and senators, I knew they were powerful and important people. They had motorcades, and reporters and cameras swarmed around them. I would see these motorcades with ten or twelve limousines, and I had a hard time focusing on my assignment because I got caught up in the celebrity of the job.

We had all kinds of celebrities coming through. I met Angelina Jolie. We talked and took a picture together. I took a photograph with Paris Hilton too. I saw Jon Stewart a bunch of times. He was always at the Capitol. I saw Mark Cuban and Jennifer Lopez and Simone Biles and the US gymnastics team. There's a photograph that officers kept of Shaquille O'Neal when he came to the Capitol. He looked like a mountain compared to the officers who were passing the wand over him at the security checkpoint. Michael Jackson's visit to the Capitol is legendary. Some officers said Michael moonwalked through the metal detector.

One day a bunch of NBA players came to the Capitol in one of those long motorcades. I think it was the members of the NBA Players Association, and they were meeting with Congress. One of the players in the group was Amar'e Stoudemire. Amar'e was a great NBA player, rookie of the year right out of high school, a six-time NBA all-star, and five times voted to the All-NBA team. I was on my post that day. I recognized him, and he recognized me. We played against each other twice when he was at Mount Zion Christian Academy in Durham, North Carolina, and I was at Surrattsville. We talked about old times and laughed about dating some of the same girls and caught up on old acquaintances. It was good to see him.

But I was letting myself get distracted by the glitz associated with the occupation. I wasn't really doing my job well. I was looking at the motorcade, and I wasn't looking for the threat. My eyes were open, but I wasn't looking at the right thing. Over time, however, I matured and began to understand more about what my job was really about. Some of it, I guess, is a function of youth. As a trainer, it's my job to bridge what the newbies learned in FLETC and what we do every day. When I talk to the young people coming onto the force, I find that they don't really look at the news.

They don't inform themselves regarding the things that are happening, including at the Capitol, that affect them. I was like them when I first came on the force. As you grow older and take on more responsibilities, things change. You start cooking for the family, and you start paying attention to what things cost. Why are eggs so expensive? You start learning about inflation. You have to deal with school systems for your kids, medical care for your family and maybe even for your parents. Your plans for the weekend become less important. You're not necessarily asking, "Where's the party at?" Life experiences make you pay attention.

One of the people who really helped me in my transition is Corey Cumberlander, who's a training officer with the Capital Police. Corey is a guy you want to hang around with anytime, but he is always serious when he is on the job. I watched his mannerisms and how he carried himself. Always on point, on task. Just the consummate professional.

Another officer I learned a lot from is Tyrone Bond. He's the guy I arrested Rivas Grogan with. Ty is from DC. I consider him a friend and a supporter. He and Corey were both in the army. Ty is about my age, and our kids are about the same age. Like Corey, Ty takes the job seriously. I love watching them talk to people. They might laugh and joke with people at the Capitol, but at the same time they are collecting information. They are human beings, and they treat other people as human beings. Too often in policing, we don't treat people as human beings. But even if Corey and Ty are dealing with some crazy people coming to the Capitol—"There's satellites following me"—they aren't dismissive. I noted that from day one, and I appreciate that.

If I learned anything from those two, it's that, as Capitol Police officers on the First Responder Unit, we are the ones who interact with the public the most. Consequently, we must learn to communicate and do it well. We could stand there like statues and not talk to anybody, like the guards at Buckingham Palace in London, or we could engage. Corey and Ty taught me that talking to people was part of our duty, and it is also a great way to look for clues of a threat. As a training officer, I tell my people the same thing.

We get 2.1 million people at the Capitol every year. So, you have to be on your toes. You have to pay attention. We get the most tourists and demonstrators when the weather is warm. We call it protest season. Most people are just tourists, but you're chatting them up because you never know, and it beats just standing around. It also works for me because I like talking with people, and it's also my way of learning about different people and what they care about.

"Hey, buddy, how's it going? What brings you to the Capitol?"

"Nice family. Oh, that's not your family?"

Or you see a demonstration. Some of it is curiosity, some of it is reconnaissance.

"Hey, I've seen that flag before. What does it stand for? Really? I never heard of that before. What is that about? Tell me about it."

Or people may be doing something wrong. You don't have to be rude. You just have to get them on the right path.

"You can't stand there. No, ma'am, I'm sorry, but that's off-limits. But you can stand over there."

People love options. People want to know what they can do, not what they can't do. Sometimes we have fun with the public. We just make up shit to have a laugh.

"Sir, what is your question? What is the statue at the top?" The real answer is that it's a nineteen-and-a-half-foot statue of a woman, called the Statue of Freedom, but . . . "That's the employee of the month," I sometimes say. "Every month they put up a new one. They're usually out of date by the time they get there, because it takes so long to make them. By that time, there's usually another employee of the month, but we leave it there for a month anyway before we put the other one up."

"The statue? One of the interesting things about the statue is that it turns. When the sun hits it in its eyes, it gradually swivels. Nobody wants the sun in their eyes. So, to keep it realistic, it turns. Keep looking and you might see it."

It's just fun and games, but those protesters and all those people, day in and day out, helped me grow in my political thinking. As we do our jobs at the hundreds of protests, we hear their slogans, we hear their chants, and you ask questions, sometimes to the people demonstrating and sometimes to yourself. Why is the minimum wage so important that you are here? Why do you think a woman's right to have an abortion is wrong? People like the late Congressman John Lewis would demonstrate, knowing they would be arrested and go to jail. We knew they were going to jail. Why would these people, business leaders, congressional men and women, activists and regular citizens, go to jail for an issue?

You talk to them. They talk to you. Somebody tells you they are taking half of their daily pill because they need to stretch it out because of the cost. Somebody else says they go to work every day, maybe work two jobs, and they still can't afford what they need. You read about what they are talking about. You stand there, demonstration after demonstration. Some people come year after year because they believe something has to change. They don't come just from DC or Maryland or Virginia. They come from all over the country because they want the people inside the Capitol to listen to them and make changes.

In the end, you understand that people need to be able to come to the US Capitol and express their displeasure. You understand that your job is to protect the rights of the people in front of you. And you also realize that we, the Capitol Police, are protecting the people inside, who have the responsibility of serving the interests and concerns of those people gathered outside, right in front of you. And you understand what you do is more than just a job. When you took the job, you took an oath to protect these people, all of them. You have a great responsibility.

You made a commitment. Now, you are obligated to make good on that commitment every day—no matter what.

3

THE INSURRECTION: PART I

In the days leading up to January 6th, most of Washington had become eerily quiet. That was especially true at the Capitol. Normally, the building and the buildings around it would have been buzzing with activity. We have thousands of people working inside and outside the Capitol: US representatives and senators and their staffs, maintenance workers, cafeteria workers, the people who run the visitors center, the tourist shops, and hundreds of Capitol Police officers. In addition, there are hundreds of people in and out during the day: tourists, lobbyists, reporters, people testifying before congressional panels, and citizens who arrive at the Capitol to talk to their local legislator.

But over the previous weeks, activity had slowed dramatically. We were still in the throes of the COVID-19 pandemic. The Capitol had pretty much shut down. Tours were halted, and legislators and their staff were mostly working remotely. It was the same for other federal departments and most city workers. Most nonresidents don't realize it, but DC is pretty much a company town. About one in three people in the city works for the federal government or a federal contractor. That's a lot of people not on the street.

In addition to the Capitol, all the other tourist attractions were closed. Nobody was coming to visit the Air and Space Museum, the African American Museum, the Portrait Gallery, the American Indian Museum, the Museum of Natural History, the zoo, or any of the other Smithsonian sites. They weren't coming for the Washington Monument, the Lincoln Memorial, or the Vietnam Veterans Memorial either. There's a lot to visit, and all those exhibits were shut down at the height of the pandemic. So, DC was empty of the thousands of people who come here every month. On top of that, most of the city government was shut down, as were most of the restaurants, coffee shops, movie theaters, and other things that residents support.

I enjoyed the silence. For months, the streets were almost deserted during my morning commute. That was particularly true in the winter because it was dark when I started rolling toward work at 6:15 in the morning. For months, there had been virtually no traffic, but as I was coming down North Capitol Street on January 6th, there were people everywhere. Everybody was walking around aimlessly. There was another group walking down Independence Avenue with their flags. I could see Trump flags, MAGA flags, and American flags. I thought, "They are starting early." It was cold, near freezing. The night before had been around thirty degrees, and it was still early in the day, so the temperature hadn't risen much above that.

I arrived at the Capitol at my normal time, 6:45 a.m., maybe 6:50 a.m., with plenty of time to spare before our 7:00 a.m. briefing. Under normal circumstances, the officers on my shift met each morning in a large room for a joint briefing. But these weren't normal circumstances. The first COVID-19 vaccine hadn't been released until a month earlier, on December 11, which meant very few Americans, particularly Capitol Police officers, had been vaccinated. We were all vulnerable to a potentially deadly disease.

We had halted the practice of joint meetings for months to avoid huge numbers of officers contracting COVID-19. January 6th was different. For one thing, anytime the vice president comes to the Capitol, it's a big deal. Not only was Vice President Mike Pence going to be there, but all the legislators were returning to certify the 2020 presidential election. So, we were, again, providing security for hundreds of people who hadn't been in the building for a while. Second, we were expecting a large demonstration.

That day we met in a large auditorium. It's the same auditorium tourists sit in when they begin their tours of the Capitol. There is a huge movie screen at the front of the room, and visitors see a film about our nation's founding before they are taken on the rest of the tour. Our supervisors read the roll, and officers looked at the schedule for their assignments. Commanders told us they expected what we call "First Amendment arrests," demonstrators who violated the rules spelled out in their permits. We went over logistics, who the overall commander would be, who the field lieutenants would be, and who would be responsible for possible arrests. They told us how many platoons of the Civil Disturbance Unit would be activated.

The Civil Disturbance Unit is our version of the military's Quick Reaction Force. They are like a strike force made up of Capitol Police officers that are deployed to quickly resolve special situations. They are the unit we depend on to handle violent crowds. We used them when a handful of demonstrators got rowdy at Donald Trump's inauguration in 2017. In addition to their training, they are especially equipped to deal with hand-to-hand fighting. They have special armaments. They wear special bullet- and knife-proof vests that protect against blunt-force objects, like a baseball bat. They wear shin guards, thigh guards, and shoulder and arm protectors. They have helmets with a clear, pull-down shield, and they carry special elongated batons.

During demonstrations, they gear up and hang back inside the Capitol, ready for when we need them. They don't appear with us so as not to antagonize the demonstrators. Having that kind of show of force insinuates that we think peaceful demonstrators are prone to violence. Imagine demonstrating to save the environment, and you've got a bunch of armored-up police staring down at you. Instead, the Civil Disturbance Unit is ready to go and pounces only at the moment they are needed. They deal with the situation and return to their duty station inside. It is pretty rare that they are called to respond, but they are ready, just in case.

Two things happened to me on January 6th that, in hindsight, I can't explain. One I saw during our briefing. The other I learned days after the insurrection.

That morning, after we had been given our guidance for the day, our supervisors told us to head over to the property area to pick up riot helmets. They had arranged Capitol Police cars and buses for some of us to go over to the property room to pick up helmets for our fellow officers. There would be a group of four or five vehicles at a time. I was assigned to one of the teams to retrieve helmets.

When I got to the property room, I went to the counter and said, "I'm here to pick up helmets for the

First Responders Unit." The officer behind the counter disappeared for a minute or two and came back with a bunch of cardboard boxes. Inside were what looked like brand-new helmets. They were black, with a see-through shield on the front that could be raised and lowered. The officer put the boxes on a dolly, and I took them back to the van. My group brought a dozen or so helmets to the station area in the basement of the Capitol, where officers could pick them up.

So, here's what's strange about that. In my then twelve-plus years with the Capitol Police, we had never been told to pick up riot helmets for an event. Never. Never, ever. And we've handled some very big and sometimes boisterous events. We didn't wear them during the Tea Party March in 2009 that I told you about earlier. The crowd for that demonstration was estimated at about seventy-five thousand people. It was a pretty rowdy crowd too. They were cursing and yelling and chanting some pretty ugly stuff. The country was in a recession. People were losing their jobs. Unemployment was going up, and people were blaming it on Washington and Barack Obama. They had pictures of Obama painted up to look like the Joker in *Batman*, and the rhetoric was off the wall. Still, nobody suggested helmets for that event.

In 2013, about thirty-five thousand people marched to the White House for the Forward on Climate demonstration. That was an orderly crowd, but still, it was fairly large. We didn't wear helmets then. We never wore them during the annual Right to Life events, which were always around fifty thousand people. We didn't wear them during the second Million Man March in 2015, another huge crowd. We didn't wear them during the 2017 Women's March the day after Trump's inauguration, and that was more than four hundred thousand people.

Don't get me wrong. I'm not suggesting that handing out helmets to us for the first time meant somebody in our command structure knew this was going to be a violent crowd and that we might come under attack. And I'm certainly not trying to suggest that somebody in our command structure even had an inkling that the crowd was going to try to breach the Capitol. None of our officers on the front line had any indication that rioters would attack us and then try to make their way into the Capitol. I just don't understand why on that particular day before that event the First Responder Unit issued helmets for the first time ever, to my knowledge.

I'd like to know why. That's all.

The second incident happened to the Civil Disturbance Units that morning. I was told that, on the morning of January 6th, at least one platoon, maybe more, was ordered *not* to wear their protective gear that day. They were told by their supervisors that they would not be a backup unit for us when things got out of hand. Instead, they were ordered to put their gear in a location outside the Capitol, and, if they needed it, they would sprint to the location, gear up, and then join the fight. In the meantime, they were told to assume positions on the perimeter with the rest of us, without their protective gear. By the way, they were never able to reach their equipment that day.

Again, I have no idea why this order was given. I am not trying to say somebody intentionally tried to make us weaker, but that order did. Anytime a unit is told to be prepared for battle but with less equipment than it normally has, they are weaker. Again, I'm just asking, "Why?"

I picked out my riot helmet and assumed my post on the east side of the Capitol at about 9:30 a.m. From where I stood, I looked directly at the US Supreme Court building and just to the right of the Library of Congress. I was armed with my M-4 carbine. The helmet was big. To give you a sense of the size, it was too big to fit into my locker. I didn't think I needed it. I placed it on a stand at my duty post and pretty much forgot about it.

Not long after I took up my post, I got a text. A friend took a screen grab of something she saw on social media and sent it. I read it and chuckled. The caption for the message read, "Jan. 6th—Rally Point—Lincoln Park." The "objective," it said, was "THE CAPITAL." Misspelled. It continued with "Trump has given us marching orders" and to "keep your guns hidden." It urged people to "bring . . . your trauma kits" and "gas mask," to "link up early in the day" in "6–12 man teams," and indicated there would be a "time to arm up."

I pretty much shrugged it off. Nobody had ever breached the Capitol, I thought, and nobody was going to try. Looking back now, that text my friend sent me seems to have foreshadowed what happened later. At the time, though, we had not received any threat warnings from our chain of command, so I had no reason to believe that violence was headed our way. As the morning progressed, the crowd on the east side started getting bigger and more animated.

A large crowd isn't necessarily a red flag for us. I had been on duty for much larger crowds than we had that day. On the east side of the Capitol, the crowd was spread out and was sort of milling around. Mixed in with them were members of the Proud Boys. You could identify them by their orange pullover hats. The Proud Boys are, in essence, an all-male, fascist street gang that promotes violence. They are so heinous that they have been banned from most social networks, including Facebook, Instagram, Twitter, and YouTube.

They are also strong Trump supporters, and Trump tacitly supports them. After an anti-racism protester, Heather Hyer, was killed in 2017 by a neo-Nazi at a white supremacist rally that the Proud Boys helped organize, Trump lamented her death by saying, "There were good people on both sides." Trump was in his first year of office.

He didn't owe any allegiance then to the Proud Boys, the neo-Nazis, or the other racists and anti-Semites. How can there be good people on both sides when one side chanted racist and vile slogans and then ran over a woman who was peacefully protesting their bigotry?

Years later, when Trump was asked to specifically denounce the Proud Boys during his 2020 presidential debate with Joe Biden, Trump responded, "Proud Boys—stand back and stand by. But I'll tell you what, somebody's got to do something about antifa and the left."

On January 6th, as I looked out at the people in front of me, "Trump" flags dotted the crowd, and many people were chanting slogans, like "Stop the steal!" and "We want Trump!" I'd seen loud crowds. I'd seen shouting crowds. This was not unusual. The demonstration was still peaceful, just Americans exercising their rights. Nothing particularly alarming. I couldn't hear or see the other rally, but I knew Donald Trump was about a mile away at the Ellipse, continuing to spread his lies about a stolen election.

The crowd was there in the first place because of Trump. After coming out of a six-hour meeting with his advisers and being told by everybody in the room that he had lost the 2020 presidential election, Trump tweeted to his followers, "Statistically impossible to have lost the 2020 Election." Another lie. Sometimes it feels as though when Trump's lips are moving, he's lying. This was at 1:42 a.m.

on December 19, when most sane people were sleeping, unless their job required them to be up. "Big protest in DC on January 6th. Be there, will be wild!" He picked January 6th because he knew Congress was set to formally certify Joe Biden's victory in the Electoral College that day.

Early that afternoon, things began to heat up. First, all our units got a dispatch over our radios that we had an "active 10-100" at the Republican National Committee nearby. A "10-100" is the police code for a suspicious package, such as a potential bomb. (The package did turn out to be a pipe bomb that was later safely detonated.) That dispatch got my attention, and I started to get more concerned, especially because the crowds on the east front of the Capitol were continuing to grow.

Around the same time, I started receiving reports on the radio about large crowd movements around the Capitol coming from the direction of the Ellipse to both the west and east fronts of the Capitol. By then, Trump had finished his speech and had riled up his followers and sent them toward us. He filled them with some more lies about how Vice President Mike Pence had the ability to overturn the election.

"But the only way that can happen is if Mike Pence agrees to send it back," Trump told them. "Mike Pence has to agree to send it back."

In response, the crowds chanted, "Send it back! Send it back!"

In the same speech, he told them their unlawful act of trying to overturn an election was actually legal and sanctioned by the Constitution.

"And think of what you're doing," he said. "Let's say you don't do it. Somebody says, 'Well, we have to obey the Constitution.' And you are, because you're protecting our country, and you're protecting the Constitution. So, you are."

Later, he gave them their send-off. "We fight like hell, and if you don't fight like hell, you're not going to have a country anymore," he said.

The crowd chanted, "Fight for Trump! Fight for Trump! Fight for Trump!"

"So we're going to, we're going to walk down Pennsylvania Avenue. . . . And we're going to the Capitol."

Trump finished his speech just after one o'clock that afternoon, but by twelve thirty, the crowd size began to surge. Then I heard urgent radio calls for additional officers to respond to the west side of the Capitol. You could hear the desperation in the voice on our police radio. Demonstrators had "breached the fence!" the voice said.

Now it was obvious that there was an active threat to the Capitol.

I strapped on a steel chest plate for protection and grabbed my M-4 to answer the request for help on the west side of the Capitol. I scrambled down the long flight of marble steps that led to my post. I grabbed two cases of water from a nearby post. Based on the radio traffic, I knew officers would need it. I just didn't know how badly. I passed the north end of the Capitol on my way to the west side. Nothing there. When I got to the west side, I immediately saw the scaffolding for Joe Biden's presidential inauguration. It had already been set up for the ceremony, which was scheduled to be in that space exactly two weeks from that day. I looked down below to my right, and I was stunned.

What I saw was like a scene from a gladiator movie. In what seemed like a sea of people, Capitol Police officers and Metropolitan DC Police (MPD) officers were fighting desperately, hand-to-hand with rioters across the west lawn. Until then, I had never seen anyone physically assault a Capitol Police officer or an MPD officer—let alone witness mass assaults against law enforcement officers. I could see rioters hitting officers with flagpoles, sticks, and metal bike racks they had torn apart. They were throwing batteries, canned food—anything they could to hurt officers.

You could hear the screaming and hollering as the battle raged on. Blood was streaming down officers' faces. They were yelling, grunting, and trying to force the rioters back. Many of them were blinded and coughing after being doused with pepper spray, bear spray, and even WD-40. It was crazy. We used the water I brought to wash the irritant out of their eyes, and then when they were good enough, they went back into the fight.

Everything was chaos and madness. Officers fighting with rioters, then getting relief. Officers heading back to the fight, then returning, because they needed their eyes and skin flushed with water to wash off the spray. At some point, the radio blasted, "Attention, all units!" The Capitol had been breached. The rioters were in various places inside the building.

I rushed into the Capitol with another officer. I can't remember his name. It's still hard to piece it all together. We first went to the basement on the Senate side because we heard that a DC police officer needed a defibrillator. After helping, I ran back to the west terrace to help officers there. With people running around the Capitol, I knew I had to get back inside.

I went through the west side entrance and ran up the stairs to the Crypt. The Crypt is a relatively cramped, large circular room right on the first floor of the Capitol, under the Capitol Rotunda. Forty large sandstone columns in the Crypt support the floor of the Rotunda above. It's not a big space, but it's the most traveled part of the Capitol because so many entrances and hallways intersect in that area. It's called the Crypt because that's where they planned to honor George Washington by burying him there. Washington had other plans, and his body remains at his home in Mount Vernon, Virginia. But it's still called the Crypt.

When I got there, I saw rioters who had invaded the Capitol carrying a Confederate flag, a red MAGA flag, and a "Don't Tread on Me" flag. I decided to stand my ground there to prevent any rioters from heading down the stairs to the lower west terrace entrance, because that was where officers were getting decontamination aid and where they were particularly vulnerable. One bunch of assholes came by, and I warned them, "Don't go down there." One of them shouted, "Keep moving, patriots!" Another fucker showed me what looked like a law enforcement badge. He told me, "We're doing this for you!" I didn't say anything, but I wanted to kick his ass. One idiot ran up on me like he was going to try to get past me and head down the stairs. I'm six feet seven and weigh three hundred pounds. I hit that sucker and knocked him down.

After a few minutes, I was relieved by other officers in the Crypt. I say a few minutes because that's what it felt like, but in situations like January 6th, I found, you lose sense of time. After the other officers arrived, I took off, running up a winding spiral staircase toward the Speaker's Lobby. Now I was on the same floor as the Rotunda. I have no idea where what little energy I had was coming from. I guess the adrenaline was pumping and keeping me going. You're not thinking. You're just reacting. You just go until you can't.

As soon as I made it to the landing, I saw Special Agent David Lazarus. He was dressed in a business suit. Other people would never know his role. He was being hassled by some rioters. Right across from where I was standing, I could read the sign above the door to an office in gold leaf and all capital letters, "SPEAKER OF THE HOUSE NANCY PELOSI." I'm guessing those idiots didn't see it.

I also saw Capitol Police officer Tanisha Ford at the top of another stairwell, just to the left of Pelosi's office. She was being harassed too. I immediately started talking to the rioters to distract them from Lazarus and Ford. I was thinking, "Y'all come over and fuck with me." I was standing in the spot where the Oath Keepers would lie during their trial later and say they defended me. They didn't defend me. I told them, like I told all the other rioters, "Get the fuck out of the building." I looked again, and Lazarus was gone. Ford had also disappeared.

I didn't know it until two days later, but while those assholes were hassling me, Lazarus snuck Pelosi's staff out of her office and into a safe space through another entrance. To this day, Pelosi and her staff greet me warmly whenever I see them because of my help.

As these assholes turned to me, I saw that some of them were dressed like members of a militia group. I'm sorry, but they were assholes to me. Every time I think of them, I get angry. Anyway, they were dressed like militia members. They had on tactical vests, cargo pants, and body armor.

By now, I was physically exhausted. It was also hard to breathe and see because of all the chemical spray in the air and on my clothes. More insurrectionists were pouring into the area by the Speaker's Lobby near the Rotunda, some wearing MAGA hats and shirts that read, "Trump 2020." I told them to get the fuck out of the Capitol.

"No, no, man, this is our house!" they yelled back. "President Trump invited us here! We're here to stop the steal! Joe Biden is not the president!"

"Yeah," another said. "Nobody voted for Joe Biden!"

I am a law enforcement officer, and I keep politics out of my job. We have to. I can't deny my feelings about Donald Trump. I didn't like him when he was elected, and I think he was a terrible president. I think he's a terrible human being, but my opinion doesn't mean a thing when I'm doing my job. When Trump came to the Capitol, I was responsible for providing a secure environment. We all were. At Trump's State of the Union speeches and at his inauguration, it was my job, all of our jobs, to keep him safe. I take my oath very seriously. That's how I'm able to do my job and protect people I fundamentally disagree with.

That's true for all of us. That sounds simple, but I want you to think about the complete picture. Imagine I'm a gay woman or man having to protect Congress people who I know don't like the fact that I am gay and would do everything in their power to take away my rights if they could. I'm a Black person protecting some Congress people who I know are bigoted and racist, and they are working to keep people like me from voting. I'm a pregnant officer who needs an abortion, and I am protecting some Congress people who want to do everything they can to take away my right to control my body. You have to overlook that. It's literally putting country before self.

Your personal politics have nothing to do with your job, but, in this circumstance, I responded to the rioters, "Well, I voted for Joe Biden. Does my vote not count? Am I nobody?" That went over with a thud. Instead of getting them to acknowledge another person's humanity, it did just the opposite.

One woman in a pink MAGA shirt yelled, "You hear that, guys? This nigger voted for Joe Biden!" Then the whole crowd, I'm guessing there were about twenty of them, joined in, screaming, "Boo! Fucking nigger!" No one had ever—ever—called me a nigger while I was wearing the uniform of a Capitol Police officer. I was stunned for a moment, but I didn't dwell on it. I couldn't. Things were moving fast, and there were other priorities.

The weird thing is that in the chaos on January 6th, you could get disoriented, and I was guarding a stairwell that had no real importance. Still, I was trying to keep them from going down the stairwell, but people had already broken through below. So, what was I protecting? They were fighting in the Crypt. But I'm there saying, "Y'all not coming here." Fortunately, a riot squad came up from behind me and took over my position and that area.

At this point, I was overwhelmed. I had pepper spray all over me. I was exhausted. I was dehydrated. The good thing was, more units were coming into the area. I saw another tactical team. They weren't Capitol Police. I don't know who they were, but they were law enforcement, which meant we were getting a bit of help. I went into Pelosi's office to make sure nobody was there. It was empty, and it was ransacked. I saw a water cooler. I grabbed one of the Speaker's fancy crystal glasses with her name on it and started downing water. I must have filled that glass eight or nine times. I also saw a large box of KN-95 masks. I used one to replace the cloth mask I had over my face. It was soaked with pepper spray and useless by now. I grabbed two boxes of masks from the bigger box and stuck them in the side pockets of my cargo pants to hand out to other officers.

I made my way to the Rotunda. The Rotunda is a large circular room that is the display room of the Capitol. It's the room that all the tourists visit when they come. It's filled with statues and ornate paintings that reflect—and sometimes distort—our nation's history. Inside the Rotunda, there was still fighting going on. Rioters were spraying the fire extinguishers into the air. The halon from the fire extinguishers stays in the air. When it mixes with the pepper spray, you're walking through a cloud of chemicals that fills the room and stays there. So, the whole room is a toxic mess. Most of the rioters were gone, but a few were left. I saw a couple of officers, and I said, "Let's get the rest of these motherfuckers out of here."

There was one particular rioter wheezing against a wall. He couldn't breathe because he was overcome with pepper spray. He's saying, "I can't breathe." An officer comes over to him and says, "Can I help you, sir?" The officer gave him a bottle of water so he could wash off some of the shit that was irritating him. I ran over and snatched the bottle out of the dude's hand and threw it halfway across the Rotunda. I said, "Fuck you. Get the fuck out." And I pushed him. These were the fuckers who were beating my fellow officers. Fuck him. Fuck all of them.

That's where I had my near-meltdown moment. By now, we were already three or four hours into the fight. I was exhausted. I sat under the huge painting at the top of the Rotunda of George Washington resigning his command to try to get myself together. Two other officers, Jonathan Sacks and Chaz Crawford, came over and sat down with me. I gave them a big hug. We're trying to catch our breath and support each other.

"You okay?"

"Yeah, you okay?"

"Yeah, I'm good."

I hugged them again and told them I love them. Maybe it was the stress, but everything started pouring out.

"I love you, brother," I said to both of them.

We were all trying to make sense of the madness. We talked about what we'd been through so far. We talked about what had been happening. They told me about what they had gone through. I shared what had happened to me. We knew we were just taking a break before we went back into the battle. The building still was not clear. Below us, people were still fighting in the Crypt.

The Rotunda is the jewel of the Capitol. I sat there surrounded by historic paintings that I usually took for granted: massive portrayals of American history and mythology, the discovery of the Mississippi River, pilgrims preparing to leave Europe for the New World, the surrender of British general Lord Cornwallis during the Revolutionary War, the baptism of Pocahontas, and what's called the Apotheosis of Washington painted inside the dome at the very top. There are huge stone statues of Martin Luther King, activist Susan B. Anthony, abolitionist Lucretia Mott, and Presidents Thomas Jefferson, Dwight Eisenhauer, Ronald Reagan, and Gerald Ford.

As I looked around, what was normally a pristine room had been trashed, bottles of liquor, drugs, discarded weapons, and other crap strewn across the floor. The air was a foul, caustic, nearly unbreathable mist.

Then everything hit me all at once. I was crying, tears streaming down my face. I hadn't processed the N-word before, but now everything was starting to sink in—the blood, the violence, the pain, the smells, the sounds, the threats, the attacks, the racism, the desecration of the nation's Capitol, and I started shouting. I couldn't help it.

"Bro, what the fuck just happened?! Can you believe this shit?! Fuck! What the fuck?! What the fuck?! What happened to our country?!"

And then I started yelling the same thing over and over.

"Is this America? Is this America?"

4

THE INSURRECTION: PART II

"What the fuck is funny?" I screamed. "What the fuck are you laughing at. Where the fuck were you? We didn't have no fucking help. Fuck y'all."

I have to admit, I lost it for a moment, but when they showed up the way they did, it just set me off.

The Rotunda was clear, and, by now, we had Capitol Police officers posted, so no one could get into the Rotunda anymore. Then, almost out of nowhere, in come these well-dressed guys in trench coats, hair slicked back, all upbeat. It's the FBI. We call them suits. They come in, all upbeat and loose. They were chatting us up.

"Hey, guys. How's it going? How's the family?"

They were chuckling and laughing at something. We've been through hell, and we've got more to go through, and these assholes think something is funny. I started hollering at them.

"Fuck y'all. Fuck y'all. Where the fuck were you?"

I'm screaming away, and Chaz grabs me.

"Harry, Harry," he said.

Captain Mendoza came over and gave me a hug. Captain Carneysha Mendoza is one of the many heroes of that day. She works out of our Special Operations division. Part of her job is as a field commander of one of the Civil Disturbance Units. She was at home eating with her ten-year-old son before her three o'clock afternoon shift when she got a call from a captain at the Capitol at about one thirty. "We need help," he told her. Two months prior, Captain Mendoza and her unit had fought with hundreds of right-wing Trump supporters, including the Proud Boys, during the so-called Million MAGA March in front of the Supreme Court. The struggles were so fierce, she told US senators later, that she could barely move the following day. After the captain's call, Mendoza rushed down to the Capitol and worked with a Civil Disturbance Unit team to secure the Rotunda. That's how I ran into her.

When she hugged me, I was crying. I was mad, distraught, and confused, all at once. I must have said "fuck" two hundred times in ten minutes. For a minute, nobody said a word. I realize now that I overreacted. I know those agents didn't mean a thing by it. They were just doing their job, but the stress and anguish of the moment just got to me.

(You, like so many people I've talked with about that day, are probably asking, "Why didn't they shoot the insurrectionists?" It's a valid question. Yes, people outside the Capitol were threatening our lives and the lives of the people we swore an oath to protect, but there are several reasons why we didn't. To quickly dispel a myth, we were never told that we could not fire our weapons. The subject actually never came up, because none of us thought the people at the Capitol that day would actually attempt to breach our lines. It had never been done, even in the most raucous demonstrations. I never imagined that I might open fire into a crowd at the Capitol.

But here's the core of the issue: Who do you shoot? If you just start firing indiscriminately into the crowd, you are at risk of killing people who are unlawfully there but who primarily are stupidly swept up in the moment. Yes, some people were there to physically harm us, but so many people weren't. They were violating the law. They were committing crimes. Should we have shot them? I didn't want to shoot those people. I didn't want to shoot anyone. None of us did. And you have to remember, at our core is our oath to protect the people inside the Capitol, but we also are there to protect Americans outside the Capitol and their right to address their government, whether we agree with them or not.

Finally, what if we had started firing and armed people in the crowd began firing at us? Then we would have had the potential for a real bloodbath with all kinds of innocent people being hurt. Fortunately, there was only one shot fired that day. Lt. Michael Byrd and other Capitol Police officers were protecting about sixty to eighty House members and staffers who were holed up inside an area of the Capitol. When Ashli Babbitt, a former member of the Air Force, and other insurrectionists tried to force their way into the room, Byrd fired his weapon. Babbitt was killed. The fact that there was only one shot fired speaks to our level of training and the caliber of our officers. Things could have been much worse. They should be commended.)

I finally got myself together, at least emotionally, but I was still a mess. We all were. Sweaty, exhausted. We were soaked in pepper spray and halon that kept reactivating and burning our eyes and skin. I ambled over to the George Washington statue, which is on the same side of the Rotunda I came in. Officers Melissa Marshall, Wayne Gibson, Jimmy Kissinger, and about three other officers all gathered around. We all agreed we had to clear the rest of the building.

"Before we do that," I said, "everybody, take out your cell phone and send your loved ones a text to let them know you're okay."

Wayne Gibson patted his pockets and looked at me blankly.

"I don't know where my phone is," he said.

"No problem," I responded. "You can use mine."

I reached for my phone, and I didn't have mine either. I realized that I had left it at my post on the east side of the Capitol when everything kicked off. I know it sounds like making those phone calls, sending those texts, was a frivolous thing to do, considering everything that was going on, but Melissa thanks me for that moment all the time. It meant so much to her family. Jimmy Kissinger's mom and dad thanked me personally, because they said there was no way Jimmy was going to make that call if I hadn't prompted him. I needed to let my family know I was okay, my mother, my father, my siblings, and especially my daughter.

So, I started back to the east side of the building. I left the Rotunda through the Senate side, swung quickly past the statue of President Andrew Jackson. As I was headed down the hall, I heard a dispatch on the radio. It said staffers were trapped in a room on the Senate side of the Capitol.

I realized that I was in the area. I checked in and told them I would respond to the call. I know Fox News and conspiracy idiots are spreading the lie that nothing really happened on January 6th, that the people inside the Capitol were just gently strolling along, but there was real, real fear among the staffers and people in that building. They were under threat, and they knew it. They knew the rioters roaming through the building wanted to harm them. That was what the people inside the room I was responding to feared. The call coming from our dispatcher said people were inside, and they had heard someone banging on the door, but they couldn't determine if it was the police or rioters. So they wouldn't open the door.

I didn't know how scared they were until I found out later that a good friend of mine, Sergeant Joe Pitts, had responded to their request for help. He was trying to get through the door to escort them to safety. They wouldn't open the door. They told him they wanted proof he wasn't a rioter. He slid his credentials under the door to prove he was legitimate.

They responded, "We're not opening the door, because you could have stolen that off an officer."

Fear. That's not made-up bullshit. That was real fear.

I checked the room, and nobody was there. The entrance was the side door to a bigger office. As I swung back into the main corridor and headed down the hall, I passed the main door and looked up at the sign. MAJORITY LEADER. It was Republican Senate Leader Mitch McConnell's office. The people under siege in the Capitol that day didn't think the rioters were just there for Democrats. They believed they were there to harm anybody and everybody.

The corridor I was on took me directly to the Senate Chamber, where the senators meet publicly to vote on bills and give speeches about pending legislation. I made a right turn as I approached the front door of the chamber and turned down the wide hall, where reporters and television crews grab senators for brief interviews before and after sessions. I hit the next corridor and turned left. I passed the area where Officer Eugene Goodman saw Senator Mitt Romney headed toward the rioters. Goodman deftly faked them into following him in the opposite direction and led them away from a man they most certainly would have harmed.

I made it out the east side and back to my post and the podium where my phone and helmet were sitting. As soon as I picked up the phone, I saw a video call coming in from my daughter, Daphne. Daphne was eleven. She was at home with her mother. She probably hadn't gotten home from school much earlier. I took my jacket sleeve and tried to clean off my face, so she wouldn't see me looking all crazy when I turned on my video. I had forgotten that my jacket and most of my clothes were covered with pepper spray and other irritants. I was in pain, but I had to hold it in and take the call.

"Hey, baby," I said in my daddy voice, as though everything were normal. "How are you?"

She didn't have a clue what was going on. She was telling me a little about her day. She was just talking. She was telling me how she made homemade ice cream. I was screaming inside from the pain, but I had to hold it together for her. Finally, I told her I had to get back to work. I'm sure her mom knew what was happening, so I sent her momma a message through my daughter that only her mother and I would truly understand.

"Gotta go, baby," I said in my upbeat voice. "Tell Mommy that Daddy's okay."

I hung up and immediately started screaming, because my eyes and face were burning. I looked at my phone, and there were a million messages. There's no way I could respond to all these people individually. So, I decided to post something on Facebook. I'm pretty active on Facebook. It's how I keep up with many of my friends, particularly the people from my days at James Madison University. I went to Facebook and posted, "I'm okay." At that point, I had to get back into the fight.

I headed back into the building, through the Senate side, to the House. I went immediately to the Crypt. It was filled with people fighting. We were pushing, shoving, grabbing rioters and getting them out of the building. We were shouting, "Fuck you! Get out of here. Get the fuck out." In some cases, we were pushing people into a bathroom and holding them there to deal with later. This is the first time that day that I saw Sargeant Gonell. He and some other officers were trying to carry a woman to a place where our medical teams could attend to her and give her CPR.

She was a big woman. She was dressed in ripped jeans and a blue hoodie. I grabbed what I could of her, but it was hard to get a grip. I still had my rifle on me, but I'm a pretty strong guy, so the four of us reconfigured our holds and kept going. We finally got her into a hallway and just outside the door of the office of Rep. Stenny Hoyer, then the House majority leader. Officer Connor Rhodes immediately began CPR.

I paused for a minute and noticed that a portrait of civil rights leader and longtime Congressman John Lewis had been ripped up and was laying on the ground. I had seen the photo before as I passed through the hall. It stood outside Hoyer's office. Hoyer put it there as a tribute to a true American hero, and he displayed it with Lewis's famous quote about getting into "good trouble."

"When you see something that is not right, not fair, not just, you have to stand up, speak up, speak out, and find a way to get in the way and get in trouble," it read. "Good trouble. Necessary trouble."

It was clear that the destruction of a photo of a Black man had been targeted. None of the other things outside Hoyer's office were touched.

I later learned that the woman I carried was Rosanne Boyland. She was thirty-four and lived in Kennesaw, Georgia, a suburban community just northwest of Atlanta. Boyland was another of those tragic figures from the madness of that day. She was most likely dead when we grabbed her and desperately tried to get her to the paramedics. We were never able to revive her. The coroner ultimately ruled that she had been crushed to death by the mob fighting at one of the Capitol entrances. A friend who was with her that day told a television reporter that she was pinned to the ground when bodies of police and protesters pushed against each other and fell on her. Her friend said he put his arm under her to pull her out and then another guy fell on top of her. He said another man was walking on her. But it has been determined that Boyland was not trampled to death but, rather, that she died from an amphetamine overdose.

Boyland had experienced her share of troubles early in life. She became addicted to drugs and had stacked up a series of drug arrests. She had been sober for several years, and she was working to keep her life on track. She was attending an addiction group in Atlanta and helping out her sister with her children by picking them up after school. Then she started listening to Trump's lies and the crazy QAnon theories about him saving the country from Democrats and liberals who were kidnapping and abusing children, even to the point of drinking their blood.

Boyland's family heard the wacky theories and tried to dissuade her, but she kept going. They just shook their heads. They loved her. She was family. What do you do? They begged her not to go to the Capitol. She promised them she would stand on the sideline and just offer visual support, but like so many people, she got caught up. And now she's dead. Dead for nothing! Her family blames her death on Trump for his lies and his call for people to come to Washington to try to overturn the 2020 presidential election so he could stay in power. And when they did that, they started receiving death threats from Trump followers.

I headed back to the Crypt. Much of the fighting had stopped. There were only a handful of people remaining there. We kept rounding up people and pushing them outside. I headed out a downstairs door. The rioters had written "Murder the Media" on the door. When I stepped outside, I was immediately hit by the weather. It was cold as fuck. It was also dark, which struck me. I had been in the Capitol, fighting, moving, helping, and dealing with so much that I had lost track of time. The last time I had been outside was to talk with my daughter that afternoon.

Even though it was dark, the outside of the Capitol was lit like a scene from the aftermath in one of those disaster movies. Floodlights, police lights, spotlights. The parking lot was filled with cars from surrounding law enforcement agencies who had come to help: the Metropolitan Police Department, Prince George's County, US Marshals, the FBI. The National Guard had taken up position, and helicopters could be heard overhead surveying the area. I linked up with other Capitol Police officers. We walked around, surveying the damage and sharing notes. Lots of hugs. The damage was considerable. Windows were broken everywhere. The building was filled with trash. Doors and furniture were destroyed.

I got a text from a buddy, Garrett. He was formerly with the Capitol Police, but he had moved on and was now working as a US Marshal. He was there assisting in the investigation and securing the site. We caught up with each other. I went back inside the building and went into Statuary Hall. Statuary Hall is another large, oval room. It is filled with statues that were donated by the states. Each state gets to have two statues in the Capitol, many of which are displayed in this room, which actually used to be where Congress met when the country was much smaller. The room was filled with officers from the various units and law enforcement departments who had fought that day. Their eyes were glazed over. Nobody was talking. They were spent and just trying to recover. Some were propped against the statues. Others were propped against each other.

We spent a few more hours checking on each other. We sat around listening to other officers talk about their feelings and what had happened. I was listening, but I wasn't hearing much. The lights were on, but I just wasn't there. I was too busy trying to process my own feelings. I clocked out shortly after midnight. It was a seventeen-hour day.

All of my friends will tell you that I love my music. If I'm in my car, the music is playing. That night, I drove home in silence. I got to the house and opened the door to the backyard so Frosty, my pit bull/boxer mix, could go outside. I walked around in a daze for a while. Just standing there. Then I moved somewhere else in the house and just stood there for a while.

I took off all my clothes. They were soaked with grime, sweat, and pepper spray. I immediately put them in the washing machine. I would get to them a day or two later. I picked up a glass to pour myself a drink. Instead, I grabbed the bottle of Weller Antique 107 and headed for the shower. There was about a third of a bottle of bourbon left. I stepped inside, bottle in hand, and turned on the water. The hot water felt good. It soothed the soreness of the bumps and bruises from the day. I just stood under the spray, drinking from the bottle. I started crying again. That's all I can remember from the rest of that night.

Drinking in the shower and crying.

5

THE DAY AFTER

On the morning of January 7, 2021, my alarm went off at its usual time: five thirty. I don't remember waking up, but I also couldn't remember falling asleep. I must have, at least for a couple hours, but the blaring of my alarm didn't jolt me awake like it usually did. It didn't "wake" me at all. My eyes were open, and I could move my body, but my mind was cloudy, as if it were lost in a fog. I had the physical pain. The bruised limbs, the ache all over my body, like I remembered from my football days. But my mind was numb.

I got out of bed and went through the motions of getting ready for my day. I never considered whether I should take the day off. As a police officer, I have to get back up. That's part of the job. It's what my fellow officers and I signed up for. I knew they'd be there, back at work, if they could be. If they could be . . . some couldn't be. And for the first time, I felt something that I would probably feel for the rest of my life: rage. It came like a sudden storm, a deep anger that filled me. Images of my fellow officers being beaten, pepper sprayed, and overrun came flooding back to me. It's not like I had forgotten about the attack, but my mind was in such a fog that to be confronted with those painful memories nearly overwhelmed me. But I had to keep going.

By six o'clock, I was in my car, driving to the Capitol in the predawn darkness. As I neared the building, I noticed other law enforcement and military personnel everywhere. I guess they probably hadn't slept at all. National Guard trucks clogged the streets, mixing with Capitol Hill cars and vehicles of several other law enforcement departments. Bright siren lights broke the morning calm, while cops and troops in riot gear patrolled the streets leading up to Capitol Hill. I drove my car to Capitol Hill Police headquarters, near the Senate Dirksen Office Building, and walked through a militarized zone to the Capitol Building. At seven o'clock, I was sitting with the other officers in the cafeteria where we held roll call. As I sat there, waiting for the day's orders, Antonio, my trainee, came bounding up to me. I had heard he had been taken out of the fight the previous day, but clearly his injuries weren't serious enough to keep him off work.

"What do we got today?" he asked me.

It was his tone that irritated me. I could barely form a coherent thought, and here was this kid, as anxious as ever to start his day. I didn't even look at him.

"Just . . . just hang out in the break room or something," I told him. I didn't talk to him for the rest of the day.

The mood in the cafeteria before roll call was somber. Usually there's laughter, jibes, the sort of stuff one would expect when a bunch of cops get together to start their day. But not this day. This day, we all just sat, shell-shocked, waiting for someone to tell us what to do. I looked around to see who was still there and noticed quickly all the faces that weren't.

Officer Brian Sicknick was just one of dozens whose fate was unknown. The last I heard, he had been taken to the hospital, as had so many others. Word would come to us throughout the day of how these officers were faring, but, at that hour, most of us knew nothing. The sergeants who got up to speak tried to revive our spirits. They applauded our heroism of the previous day, urging us that now was the time to stick together, that we couldn't let our shock overwhelm us. We still had a job to do. There were murmurs of dissent from the group, but most of us, I imagine, just wanted to get on with it. I know I did. I just wanted to be alone.

When roll call was over, I headed to the Rotunda, walking up the very steps I had defended eighteen hours earlier. Snapshots of the fight came to my mind. I suddenly saw the corridors and corners of the battlefield, still strewn with debris and graffiti. Disgusted, I took out my phone and recorded the damage and filth that had been left under the Capitol Dome. There were batteries, placards, Trump flags, trash, and, strangely, lots of pistachios. Seriously, there were bags of pistachios everywhere. I panned my camera through the carnage, stopping at one of the entrances, known as the Memorial Doors, in honor of two Capitol Hill Police officers who were gunned down near them in 1998.

Scrawled across the window panes were the words "Murder the Media." Did the insurrectionist who wrote those words know what those doors signified? Did the others who ran rampant through the Rotunda, beneath a dome that had been erected during the Civil War when Americans had killed Americans by the thousands, appreciate their desecration? I felt that rage bubble up inside me again, a kind of hopeless anger that made me question everything. Did this building, it's purpose and its history, mean nothing to these people? How could you call yourself an American and destroy the very symbols of what makes us unique in this world?

None of it made sense to me, and that only deepened my anger. I eventually retreated to an empty room, where I didn't have to see anyone. Burying my head in my hands, I cried. Someone might have seen me; I don't recall. But I also didn't care. I was falling into a state of mind that would consume me for months. Fueled by anger but crippled by sadness, I felt helpless. I snapped my Beats by Dre headphones on and lost myself in my music while I finally responded to the dozens of texts and Facebook messages I had received since the previous day. I didn't spend much time answering each one. Instead, I opted for a quick response.

"I'm safe, but not okay." That's how I spent most of that day, sitting alone, listening to music, and replying to messages. I did venture outside at certain points to make sweeps of the grounds, where we found bullets and fire-crackers. Then I retreated back to an empty conference room and resumed my isolation. Bouts of sobbing would suddenly hit me, as my anger overtook my emotions. I wanted to scream, but instead I just cried.

As a group, we didn't discuss much about who was at fault for the chaos during the attack—at least not that day. I didn't have firm feelings on this one way or the other that morning, but, as the day wore on and I started looking at the news, my anger turned toward our Capitol Police leadership. I thought they had let us down, leaving us on our own for too long to control a situation that, from the very beginning, was entirely out of hand. I don't necessarily think that way anymore, but, at the time, when I was looking for someone to blame, I couldn't help it. And others were thinking the same thing. By the early afternoon, I saw that Speaker Pelosi had called on our police chief, Steven Sund, to resign.

My initial thought was "Good! Someone has to answer for this." When Chief Sund eventually offered his resignation later that evening, my temper had cooled a bit. I didn't really blame him, but I felt that he was doing the honorable thing by taking responsibility. In the months to come, we would all learn more about what happened and why, but, at that moment, not even twenty-four hours after the battle, everyone was confused and in shock—the Capitol Police most of all. All throughout that day, I remained locked away, occasionally chatting over group texts to fellow officers but having no desire to be in anyone's presence but my own. I was counting the minutes until I could just go home when an email suddenly came through my inbox. It was from LinkedIn.

"What the fuck is LinkedIn?" I asked the empty conference room. Then I remembered.

Nearly ten years earlier, when I had been job hunting, I had opened a LinkedIn account to help my search. The Capitol Police job came to me shortly afterward, so I never ended up doing anything with my profile. I hadn't even looked at it in a decade. So, I was wondering why someone named Emmanuel Felton was trying to reach me through that long-ignored account.

His message to me was simple enough. "Are you a Capitol Hill Police officer?" he wrote. "I'd love to talk to you about what happened."

What the hell was this? I clicked through to his profile: "BuzzFeed reporter." Ah. Then I saw that he was Black. That helped a lot, making me feel like this guy might get it. Without thinking through any of the ramifications, personal or professional, I replied, "Yeah, what's up?"

And that started the conversation that would change my life.

I learned Brian Sicknick died later that night, at around nine thirty. The group text I was on with other officers got the news before anyone else. The true nature of Brian's death wouldn't be fully known for several weeks, but, at that point, news of his passing only added fuel to the gradually growing fire that was within me. The few conversations I had had with others on January 7 and the days following broke down along two camps: There were those who, like me, were in a state of shock, disbelief, and anger at what had happened—and been allowed to happen. I even spoke to officers who had been Trump supporters who felt this way. "Trump was responsible for my friend [Sicknick] being dead, and I'll never forgive him for that," one officer, who I would describe as a hardcore Trump supporter, told me.

But there was another sentiment I heard expressed at this early stage, when even most of the Republican caucus had condemned the violence. "Was it really that bad? What's the difference between this one and other protests we've had?"

The presence of the first sentiment—by full-on Republicans no less—did little to dampen my rising rage at those who expressed the second view. Throughout my life, I have rarely made knee-jerk decisions. I have always attempted to hear the other side of an argument and make sure that when I come to an opinion, it's an informed one. I might not agree with you, but I'll listen to you.

But no matter how hard I tried, I simply couldn't understand the view of my fellow officers who seemed to be dismissing the attack on January 6th. I wanted to scream at them, "Did you go through the same shit I did?" They all agreed that it shouldn't have happened, but they also refused to condemn the attack as anything more than a peaceful protest that got out of hand. Of course, this was completely different from the experience I had—when I had been fighting through hallways and stairwells against a mob that knew what it was doing. They knew why they were there. They even told me. That anyone could dismiss it as anything other than a concerted assault enraged me.

And it was this mentality that I carried into a conversation with Emmanuel Felton from BuzzFeed. We exchanged a few more messages that evening and into the next day. My early messages to him were evasive. I knew what he was asking me to do, but I was pretty damn sure I shouldn't be doing it. There was still graffiti on the Capitol walls. There was still trash in the corridors. People had died. Dozens of my fellow officers were in the hospital, some with critical injuries. I knew that for these reasons, I shouldn't start mouthing off to a reporter. Forget the professional consequences; there were also the personal relationships I might tarnish. You go through battle together only to then start talking about the experience with someone who wasn't there? It didn't feel right.

But then there was my anger . . . and my extreme sadness. Combined, these two emotions triggered in me a need to say something. No one has ever had to wonder what I'm thinking. And at that moment, I was thinking that there were several groups of people who had failed my fellow officers and me at our most dangerous moment. And so, as my conversation with Felton continued, I became less resistant, and we started to discuss how we could keep me anonymous if I did grant him an interview.

Felton assured me he would protect my identity, but, as we talked, I realized that I needed to make a decision. If I spoke with him, there would be a good chance I would be identified. My fellow officers know me. My superiors know me. They knew I had trouble keeping my mouth shut. They knew I was struggling with the attack. Given the details I would give Felton, it wouldn't take a Sherlock Holmes to finger me as the source. So, if I was going to do it, then I had to be okay with being identified and perhaps losing my job. And then, I suddenly realized, I didn't care anymore. "Fuck it," I said to myself. "This is bigger than me."

When Felton and I actually conducted the interview over the phone, a sudden change came over me. Perhaps it was just the pent-up frustration and anger that I had been dealing with for the last two days. Or maybe it was that Felton, a Black man, also saw the racial component to January 6th—one that so many in the media seemed to be ignoring entirely. Felton had purposefully reached out to Black officers because he wanted to hear the experience of Black cops fighting against white rioters. It's usually the opposite, as the nation witnessed the previous summer (not to mention for many decades). This was a guy who got it. And so I didn't hold back in the slightest. Felton is a reporter, but being able to tell my side of the story to anyone had a cathartic effect on me, much like I was talking to a therapist.

Did I feel better afterward? That's hard to say. My anger was still there and would only increase as the months went by, but I felt relieved, as though, for a brief moment, a weight had been lifted. I also felt like myself again, more than I had since before January 6th.

BuzzFeed published Felton's article on January 9 under the headline, "Black Police Officers Describe the Racist Attacks They Faced as They Protected the Capitol." It wasn't the first in-depth account of what happened, but it did provide the perspectives and experiences of two Black officers who were there that day, a veteran and a younger man, as Felton described me and my fellow officer. (To this day, the other officer remains anonymous.) It doesn't take a deep reading to see how I had let loose my anger to Felton:

> The officer even described coming face-to-face with police officers from across the country in the mob. He said some of them flashed their badges, telling him to let them through and trying to explain that this was all part of a movement that was supposed to help.
>
> "You have the nerve to be holding a Blue Lives Matter flag, and you are out there fucking us up," he told one group of protesters he encountered inside the Capitol. "[One guy] pulled out his badge, and he said, 'We're doing this for you.' Another guy had his badge. So I was like, 'Well, you gotta be kidding.'"

And then Felton reported on the angle I felt so many in the media had been missing. He wrote,

> While it was a hard day for almost every officer at the Capitol, Black officers were in a particularly difficult position, he said, and he drew a stark

contrast with how police handled the Black Lives Matter protests [the previous] summer.

"There's quite a big difference when the Black Lives Matter protests come up to the Capitol," he said. "[On Wednesday], some officers were catering to the rioters."

He said that what upset him the most was when he later saw images of a white Capitol Police officer taking a selfie with the attackers, seeming to enjoy his time with the insurrectionists who were roaming the US Capitol with Confederate flags and other symbols of white supremacy.

I unloaded my frustration with Capitol Hill Police Chief Steven Sund.

Felton quoted me anonymously as saying, "Our chief was nowhere to be found, I didn't hear him on the radio. One of our other deputy chiefs was not there. . . . You don't think it's all hands on deck?"

I was wrong when I said that. You have to remember, it was less than twenty-four hours after the trauma of January 6th. So, the pain was fresh, and my thoughts were scattered. I found out later that the chief was in the tunnel, coordinating getting us help. He was doing his job. I just couldn't see it.

You can also tell that I took my "fuck it" attitude into the interview, since I let slip this nugget, describing my actions after the attack had ended: "I sat down with one of my buddies, another Black guy, and tears just started streaming down my face," Felton quoted me as saying. "I said, 'What the fuck, man? Is this America? What the fuck just happened? I'm so sick and tired of this shit.'"

Felton then described how I was screaming, so that everyone in the Rotunda, including my colleagues, could hear what I had just gone through.

"These are racist-ass terrorists," he quoted me as shouting.

There were only so many officers who others had seen crying in the Rotunda that night, and only one who screamed out that last line. My anonymity wasn't helped by the fact that Felton's article went viral, garnering tens of thousands of likes on Twitter. He would say to me later that no article of his had ever received anything near that amount of attention. He also told me that he was fielding dozens of requests from fellow journalists to disclose the identities of the two officers.

Back at work, it was an open secret that I was one of Felton's sources. And nothing happened, at least not directly to me. While I remained anonymous to the general public, I didn't hide from my fellow officers. Perhaps in less hectic times, I would have been in trouble for talking—although it's not like I leaked anything. But there were serious matters confronting our leadership—a new chief, an internal investigation about the attack, and questions about the force's response. It seemed that one lowly officer's opinion—shared by many on the force—didn't rise to the level of an urgent matter. For which I was, of course, grateful.

Then, on Twitter, I noticed that my member of Congress, Rep. Jamie Raskin, had tweeted out one of my quotes from the article. I was overjoyed. Of course, Raskin had no idea who I was, but suddenly my anonymity seemed like a hinderance. He should know who said that. He should know that it was one of his constituents who stood his ground that day. So, not thinking much of it, I called Raskin's office and told the receptionist that I was the Capitol Hill Police officer quoted in the Buzz-Feed story.

"Wait, seriously?" the receptionist asked.

"Yes, I'm Harry Dunn," I replied.

"Can you hold on just a moment, Officer Dunn?"

"Of course."

I then heard them frantically trying to figure out where Rep. Raskin was. There was a lot of commotion in the background before the receptionist got back on the line and asked for my cell number because the member of Congress would call me privately. I happily gave it, which is how I ended up having lunch not long afterward with Raskin, breaking my anonymity wide open but also talking to the lead impeachment manager for Trump's second impeachment trial. Without using my name, a few weeks later, Raskin stood in the Senate chamber and recounted a portion of my comments from the Felton article into the record of the trial.

I started to see something happening, something I never imagined would involve me. I was slowly but surely making my presence felt. That's never been a problem for me in a room full of people. People know I'm there. But in the halls of Congress, during the impeachment of an American president, I had shoved my six-feet-seven frame through those doors (metaphorically speaking), and people were now listening.

Before the impeachment trial, Felton asked if I wanted him to release my name to any of those reporters who had been asking about me. He explained that they too would protect my anonymity if I requested it. It was up to me if I wanted to continue on this media train.

"Let me think about it," I told him.

I trusted Felton, and so I trusted that he wouldn't give my name to hack journalists or those who would abuse me somehow. I wasn't the most media-savvy person—hell, I had agreed to be an anonymous source without discussing it with anyone else. I was diving headfirst into a world I knew nothing about, especially about the dangers that awaited me.

But I also knew how I felt after my interview with Felton—and certainly after seeing the incredible response the article generated. The article had done something. While the politicians and pundits were separating into their partisan camps, each trying to turn their version of January 6th into the accepted version, I had been able to tell my story, a story that represented so many of my fellow officers. That felt good. That felt like I was helping. My anger had not subsided in the least, but I was at least doing something with it. Why not continue to do something?

I called Felton back. "Okay, you can give my name to five journalists you trust," I told him. Felton thanked me and got to work. Why five? For no other reason than it seemed a manageable number to me. I had no idea what I was doing or how any of this worked. While I wanted to keep pushing the true story of January 6th, I also had a job, one that was taking up more and more of my free time. So many officers hadn't been able to return to work even weeks after the attack, and we also temporarily lost a hundred more who tested positive for COVID-19. Not only did we have to deal with the fallout of the attack, but we also had an inauguration coming up for Joe Biden. The National Guard was still on hand leading up to the ceremony on January 20, but most of us were pulling double shifts and being worked to the bone.

It speaks to the caliber of our officers that we hung together during these first couple weeks after the attack. Much like soldiers whose combat experience binds them together more strongly than ever, we all had shared something truly traumatic, an event that had taken the lives of several officers, even if only indirectly. We stood by each other during a time when our vulnerabilities had been exposed to the entire world. The threats continued to pour in as well, keeping all of us on edge as we neared Inauguration Day. As it happened, the event was peaceful—and so damn welcome. I spent the ceremony on the east side of the Capitol, and so I couldn't see President Biden take the oath of office, but I watched it on my phone—and wept.

Meanwhile, Felton had connected with five—and only five—journalists. Some, I soon discovered I wasn't interested in going forward with. The deaths of Brian Sicknick from stroke and Howard Liebengood from suicide dominated a lot of the media conversation in the weeks after the attack, but I never felt comfortable discussing my fallen officers. I was happy to give my story and walk a journalist through my experience, but I was going to hold the line at talking about someone else.

One of the journalists Felton introduced me to was Victor Ordonez, a producer for ABC News. Through Ordonez, I met Pierre Thomas, an award-winning television journalist once named Journalist of the Year by the National Association of Black Journalists. Thomas wanted to put me on air, in front of millions of viewers, to tell my story.

"What do you think?" he asked me.

Hell, I had no idea.

My interview with Felton helped me remember the therapeutic value of talking about the trauma that I had experienced. But I don't want to give the impression that I was getting better during the days and weeks after the attack when I freely let my views of January 6th be known, whether I was talking with a journalist or with anyone else. I was still racked with anger and sadness.

When I arrived at work each day, I would wait as long as I could in my car before getting out.

During lunch, when I used to love to kick back with my friends in the break room of the Capitol, instead I went back to my car and ate alone. I rarely saw friends; I avoided my family. I kept in touch with folks over text and Facebook, but that was as close as I wanted to be with anyone.

If I recognized that I was depressed, I wasn't doing much about it. I was trying to carry on, shoulder the burden of my mental anguish, as I felt a man is supposed to do. For a guy as gregarious and outspoken as I am, I discovered how quickly I turned inward when faced with true emotional trauma. I became, in essence, a different person. I was full of rage, especially as the weeks went by and it became apparent that the Republicans were walking away from their earlier condemnation of the attack, of their distancing from Trump. I found it hard to contain my feelings. Congress members I had known for years, whom I had guarded and protected through State of the Unions, inaugurations, and just the daily routine of working on the Hill, had suddenly turned on me. I couldn't understand it—I still don't. It angered me that loyalty to a single individual could overwhelm otherwise decent people—people who had fallen into the darkness and forgotten their oaths of office.

So, obviously, I wasn't in a good place for much of those early weeks after the attack. Fortunately, dealing with extreme mental trauma isn't anything new to law enforcement, and there was help available to me. Agencies all over the country sent in "peer support" officers, which was one of the best things that happened. There's nothing too special about these folks, aside from the fact that they too are law enforcement who had been through some shit before. They aren't therapists; they aren't professional trauma counselors—but they have the one thing that few of those others have: they know what you are going through because they've been through it.

I didn't sit on a couch and talk to them. They'd hang around the break room and lunch areas, just chatting with anyone who wanted to talk. Often we didn't even talk about January 6th. Sometimes I'd just listen to them tell their own stories. And so, when I spoke, I knew I was speaking to someone who appreciated the anger inside me. They had been let down by colleagues; they had lost dear friends; they had felt abandoned by their leadership. They knew what I was thinking, even if I wasn't saying it.

I'm not saying that these officers cured me, but they gave me just enough to get me through my day.

Officers like Eddie Morales, a US Marshal, came down from New York just to sit in our break rooms and listen to me blabber. Man, Eddie was a good dude. The department also has an employee assistance program (EAP) that connects officers with counselors to discuss anything that's on their mind. I wouldn't say it's a substitute for professional therapy, more like a starter kit. One of the things an EAP counselor can do is connect someone with an actual therapist.

It's a good and necessary program, and I had used it before January 6th. I knew enough about mental health to know that I needed to see an EAP counselor after the attack. Where the "peer support" officers offered a buddy to talk to, an EAP counselor could actually give some sound health care advice. I knew I was struggling, and I wanted to make use of anything available to me. Only, after leaving the EAP's office, after venting and raving for an hour to the person in the chair, I'd be angrier than before. I don't think it was the counselor's fault; I just needed a different kind of solution than talking to someone in a room by myself.

Maybe that's what led me back to Pierre Thomas and his offer of a televised interview. Talking about what was going on inside my head was good for me; I had to keep talking, keep getting those terrible thoughts out in the open. That's how I've always handled my problems, and I had to realize that my isolation was doing me more harm. I also had to reckon with the fact that handling my trauma personally and with a few confidants and professionals wasn't enough. I had to do more. The problem was that the attack on January 6th wasn't a single event. Yes, that was what primarily fueled my rage and despair, but the ongoing aftermath was just as awful. With the second impeachment of Donald Trump under way, it became clear to me that the Republican Party had no intention of holding anyone responsible for the attempted insurrection.

With each passing day, it felt like I was being told that what happened on January 6th was all in my imagination. Or that, if it was that bad, then it was the fault of nameless, random wingnuts who got a little too carried away.

Bullshit.

I fought with these insurrectionists. I spoke with them. I know what they wanted to do, and I know who sent them. And what made it all worse was that I was hearing these lies from the Americans I protected that day. We held our ground so that they could get away without casualty. They stood behind us as we faced the attackers. And now these Americans stood on the floor of the very Senate chamber that we had protected when a terrorist mob rampaged through the Capitol and voted to acquit Trump?

At the time, less than a month after the attack, I felt like those behind the attempted insurrection were going to get away with it. There weren't enough therapists or counselors in the world to overcome the mental anguish that would have befallen me if these bad actors got away with it. But my interview with Felton taught me an invaluable lesson. I didn't have to sit back and just take it. I could act myself. I could tell my story. I could do something. And so, I would.

Following Felton's article, I spoke with a colleague and revealed that I was one of the anonymous sources. He said he was proud of me, but he also gave me my first warning about the dangerous new world I was basically walking blindly into. I had entered the political arena, he said. By putting myself out there, I had ceased to be just a police officer. I was suddenly a tool (or a weapon) that either side could try to use.

He was essentially telling me that if I was going to put myself out there—even anonymously—I had to have protection. I had to have a lawyer. These were all things that I hadn't considered, and now that I was considering them, I suddenly saw how vulnerable I was. Fortunately, my colleague had someone in mind, which is how I first met Mark Zaid, a lawyer who represents whistle-blowers in government, which, in a way, I was.

It was Mark who negotiated with Ordonez and Thomas and the rest of the ABC team to arrange a televised interview that would be aired on *Good Morning America* on February 22, 2021. I don't know what in the world I would have done had I tried to do it myself. The questions Mark made me think about—the whole structure of the interview and the kind of questions that I could be asked—had never entered my mind. The negotiations also involved the Capitol Hill Police for obvious reasons. They would allow me to do the interview, as long as it was made clear that I was speaking only for myself and not for the whole department. Fine by me.

I spent an entire day with Pierre, not only sitting down for the interview but also walking around the Capitol grounds. Much of the story I told during the interview itself I had already told to Felton, but this time there was a real face behind that story. And I wanted all of America to see that face and hear my words. I was still angry, but I was now on the path of fighting back. I wasn't going to sit idly by while racists, conspiracy theorists, or the nation's elected leaders—whether they be in New York or New Mexico, Washington state or Washington, DC—bent their knees to Trump.

At one point in the interview, Pierre pointed out how I used the word *terrorists* to describe the people who stormed the Capitol.

"Absolutely," I said. "Absolutely. It wasn't just a mob or a bunch of thugs. They were terrorists. They tried to disrupt this country's democracy. That was their goal. And you know what?" I then turned to the camera. "Y'all failed."

That last little bit, while it might seem like I was over-doing it, was nothing less than how I felt. And still feel. While I wanted the rest of America to hear my story and see the human being behind that story, I also wanted the terrorists who attacked us that day to hear it as well.

That, to me, was therapy. That was using my anger for something useful. I still had a long way to go before I felt normal again, or as normal as I will ever feel, but I now understood what I had to do to get there. I had to stand up and fight back. I had to use my voice.

Afterward, when the lights had dimmed and the cameras had stopped rolling, I spent a few quiet moments talking to Pierre.

"Man, I was really nervous," I admitted to him.

"Why?" he asked.

"Because everyone knows who I am now," I said. "Everyone is going to see me as representing Black people or representing the Capitol Hill Police or representing the resistance to Trump. That makes me nervous."

"Look," said Pierre carefully. "This is your story. You represent yourself. That's all you need to worry about."

The alarm went off in my head. I was finally awake and ready to fight back.

6

OUR BLUE LIVES DIDN'T MATTER

I speak to a lot of organizations and groups these days about what happened on January 6th. It's part of my goal to deliver and grapple with the truth of what happened that day. I have spoken at high schools, colleges and universities, and events, sometimes alone and sometimes with officers Michael Fanone, Aquilino Gonell, and Daniel Hodges. Not too long ago, the four of us were at a question-and-answer session at Montgomery College in Germantown, Maryland. Not long after that, I spoke at an awards dinner in Newark, New Jersey, before the African American Chamber of Commerce.

In early March 2023, I spoke at Principles First, a three-day conference of leading conservatives and Republican and Democratic politicians. It was held at the Conrad Hotel, a swanky hotel in downtown DC, where the rate for a room with a king-size bed runs about $440 a night during the week. I had attended the conference in 2022 and was awarded the Principles in Courage Award. It was truly an honor. In 2023, Michael Fanone got the award, and I went there in support of him, but, at the last minute, they also had me participate in a panel discussion.

They had some distinguished people there, including Maryland governor Wes Moore, a Democrat; Republican Rep. Adam Kinzinger; former Maryland governor Larry Hogan, a Republican; former Ohio governor John Kasich; Alyssa Farah Griffin, a host on *The View*; and John Bolton, the former US ambassador to the United Nations under President George W. Bush and former national security adviser for a year under Donald Trump. They had conservative columnists, like Mona Charen and Bill Kristol, and they had election officials to talk about the importance and safety of our electoral system, including Arizona secretary of state Adrian Fontes and Stephen Richer, the elections recorder for Arizona's biggest county, Maricopa.

None of these Republicans, by the way, are election deniers. In fact, Hogan, who everyone thought would run for president, decided not to that weekend in a big announcement in the *New York Times* and on *Face the Nation* because he was afraid it would just help Trump win the nomination again.

I was on a panel called "Truth and Order: Keeping the Peace after January 6th." We discussed some new things, but we went over a lot of the testimony I gave before the January 6th Committee and the thoughts I have shared on other occasions. Sometimes, when people ask me how I feel about what happened to me and the other officers on January 6th, I think about the deep, painful betrayal we all feel, and that brings me to Isaac Woodard. You have probably never heard of Woodard. I hadn't heard of him either, until a friend told me about him. I looked him up and then I watched a documentary about him.

Woodard was a World War II veteran from Goldsboro, North Carolina. In February 1946, he was heading home a few hours after being honorably discharged at Camp Gordon in Augusta, Georgia. He was a sergeant. He served in the Pacific theater during the war. He enlisted in the US Army in 1942. So, he had been away for a long time. I'm guessing he was pretty excited to be going home to be reunited with his wife and the rest of his family.

Woodard was riding at the back of a Greyhound bus, because that is where Black people traveling through the South sat in 1946, no matter what they had done for their country. He proudly wore his green army uniform. Three stripes on each arm showed his rank. He had four medals pinned on his chest. There was a Good Conduct Medal, an American Campaign Medal, a World War II Victory

Medal, and a battle star Asiatic-Pacific Campaign Medal. He was awarded the last one for bravery.

When the bus arrived at a rest stop in a South Carolina town now known as Batesburg-Leesville, Police Chief Lynwood Shull and his officers dragged Woodard off the bus. The bus driver hadn't liked the way Woodard asked to use the restroom fifty-four miles back, outside of Augusta. So, when the bus got to the town, the driver called the police, even though he and Woodard hadn't shared two words since that stop.

The police demanded to see Woodard's discharge papers. Then the cops forced him into an alley, where they beat him savagely. For good measure, the police chief used his baton to gouge Woodard's eye sockets until both eyeballs ruptured beyond repair. Woodard was blind from that day forward. He was twenty-seven. And remember, all this happened while he was wearing the very uniform that identified his service to his country.

Just imagine. This man had fought faithfully for America. He had spent every day of his last four years protecting this country, and his reward was to be beaten and blinded by the very people he had put his life on the line to protect.

Now, multiply that betrayal by two thousand times, because that's how many Capitol and Metropolitan Police Department officers were viciously assaulted by Americans whose democracy we defend every day. All the

Capitol Police officers there that day had taken the same oath I took thirteen years earlier, to protect our nation from "all enemies, foreign and domestic."

And, on that day, we were betrayed by our president, many of our elected officials, and thousands of other Americans we had sworn to protect.

We were beaten. We were tased. We were stomped and stabbed. Officers had cracked ribs and smashed spinal disks. Some of our injuries required stitches. Some needed staples. Some of us suffered traumatic brain injuries. One officer lost the tip of his right index finger. Another was blinded in one eye. Some officers' shoulders were dislocated, and there were numerous concussions. Metropolitan Police officer Michael Fanone was burned with a stun gun and suffered a heart attack. He also has traumatic brain injury. Sergeant Aquilino Gonell required surgery on his shoulder and his left foot. His wounds were so severe that he retired from the force.

Capitol Police officer Brian Sicknick collapsed after the attack. Sicknick was rushed to the hospital. He suffered two strokes and died twenty-four hours later. In all, about 140 of us—73 from the Capitol Police and 65 from the Metropolitan Police Department—were injured that day. On top of that, at least 38 of us tested positive for the coronavirus right after the attack. Nearly 200 National Guard personnel who were deployed to protect the Capitol in the weeks after the siege also tested positive for COVID-19. I mention that because we got it at a particularly dangerous time. The first vaccines had just been made available three weeks earlier, and it was still difficult, back then, to get a shot.

What happened that day was unprecedented, not just in Washington or at the Capitol. Nothing like that had ever happened anywhere in any of the fifty US states since the country was founded. Never.

Unfortunately, what most people don't understand about January 6th is that the people who had gathered outside the Capitol with their flags and chants weren't trying to protect democracy. They weren't there to save America. They weren't there to "stop the steal." That day was never about politics or a political movement. If it were, where is it now?

There has been no organized follow-up to that day, just a handful of lying election deniers and politicians who ran for office hoping a nod from Trump would help get them elected.

What assembled that day was a murderous mob out for blood and destruction. A lot of them said they were there because Trump had invited them. "Be there, will be wild!" he told them in a tweet. In other words, he had invited them to come to Washington to act out. And that's what they did. All that rhetoric about patriotism was bullshit. It had nothing to do with what happened that day. It wasn't a demonstration that "got out of control," as some in the media and Congress said. They wanted to hurt people and they wanted to destroy things, plain and simple.

The insurrectionists showed their true colors as they marched to the Capitol from the Ellipse, where Trump had riled them up. As soon as they heard that the vice president wasn't going to try to overturn the election, they started chanting, "Hang Mike Pence. Hang Mike Pence." We could hear them as we stood at our posts at the Capitol. There wasn't a damn thing peaceful about that.

Then they built gallows with a noose on the Capitol grounds as a symbol of their intentions. Was that a peaceful protest? Consider this. They had already designed and cut the pieces to make the structure days before they arrived in Washington. They brought the precut wood, the rope and nails, and the tools they used to assemble it with them from their hometowns. Violence was their goal from the beginning.

As they were threatening the vice president, one said, "You fucking politicians are going to get dragged through the streets." They destroyed television cameras and other equipment that belonged to the media covering the event. They attacked reporters. While they were doing it, one of them said, "Got the lying media. Start making a list. Put all their names down, and then we start hunting them down, one by one."

This mob outside the Capitol was supposedly made up of true red-white-and-blue Americans who believe in law and order, who believe in backing the police. You know, "Blue Lives Matter" and "Protect the Blue." Not that day.

"Fuck you, police!" "Fuck the blue!" That is what they shouted at us.

Probably half the people we fought off that day were drunk. That's right, drunk "patriots." The media hasn't reported much about that. I smelled the alcohol on them. All of us did. They needed their liquid courage. It wasn't just us who saw they were drunk. Some of my friends in the DC Fire Department said they smelled it as they waded through the crowd, trying to save lives and get wounded and sick people to the hospital. This was even before the rioters tried to break into the Capitol. When we cleaned up the Capitol after the insurrection, we found liquor and wine bottles scattered throughout the building.

Many of those who weren't drunk were high on drugs. One of them was videotaped walking through the Rotunda, smoking a joint. Another rioter, Roseanne Boyland, was taken to the hospital, where she, unfortunately, died from an overdose of amphetamines. So many people were getting injured by the other rioters that the fire department was using the bike racks we used for barriers as makeshift stretchers to carry the injured out of the crowd.

Kevin Greeson was one of the casualties. Greeson left his home in Athens, Alabama, his wife, and his five children, and traveled 730 miles to Washington, DC, and died of a heart attack on the sidewalk west of the Capitol while talking to his wife on a cell phone. When I think about his story, it saddens me. Here was a man who, years earlier, came to the White House for the inauguration of the nation's first Black president. He had been a union leader.

But he bought the Trump lies about a stolen election and joined the rioters spouting violence and anger at the Capitol. Not long after Trump lost the 2020 election, Greeson wrote online, "I see nothing wrong with taking it back with guns." On December 17, less than a month before his death, he wrote online, "Let's take this fucking country BACK! Load your guns and take to the streets!" And now he was dead, hundreds of miles away from his family and people who loved him because he believed the lies of a man who didn't give a damn about him.

The truth is, the insurrectionists could have gotten past us and gone inside and occupied the Capitol, if that's what they really wanted. That's true of any of the huge demonstrations we've had over the years. I didn't say it would be easy, but two thousand officers just can't hold back tens of thousands of people. But on January 6th, most of the insurrectionists didn't go inside because they were too busy fighting with us.

They weren't trying to run around us. They were trying to take our lives. They wanted to cause damage. Some in the mob would attack one officer, then turn to attack another, and then turn to attack another. They ripped the gas masks off officers, sprayed their faces with WD-40 or bear spray, then pushed the masks back on their faces and covered the filter to force the officers to breathe in the fumes.

When they attacked Michael Fanone, they tased and beat him repeatedly, even though he was on the ground. They weren't trying to get past him and into the Capitol. That's not what they were trying to do at all. Instead, they continued to beat him, and one of them said to the others, "Kill him. Kill him with his own gun." One of the rioters jerked off Daniel Hodges's mask and shouted, "You will die on your knees."

Let me tell you about just one bunch, so you can see what I'm talking about when I say most of them were there for blood, and blood alone. Jeffrey Sabol, Justin Jersey, Mason Joel Courson, Peter Francis Stager, Jack Wade Whitton, Logan James Barnhart, and Ronald McAbee have all pleaded guilty to beating police officers and are scheduled to be sentenced. Michael Lopatic was involved in the same attack. His attorney said he was planning to plead guilty, but he died before he could. Another one of the bunch, according to the Justice

Department, was Clayton Ray Mullins, who was still awaiting trial as of July 2023.

One of them, Jersey, was sentenced to fifty-one months in prison and thirty-six months of supervised probation after his release. He also has to pay restitution of more than $32,000. I'm guessing the others will get pretty much the same.

This group came from all over: Arkansas, Colorado, Georgia, Florida, Kentucky, Michigan, and Tennessee. Ignorance and brutality are not the province of one state or region. Each came to DC with plans to inflict injury.

Sabol flew in from Colorado with a helmet, steel-toe boots, zip ties, a radio, and an earpiece. Sabol told the FBI after he was arrested that he only came to Washington to hear Trump's speech. Zip ties are what we use to restrain arrestees when we run out of handcuffs. What was he going to do with zip ties at a speech? When Sabol admitted his guilt, he told officers he "had to be on the front line" of the "battle" because he is a "warrior."

Jersey texted someone the night before the insurrection, "If anything were to happen, tell my daughter I love her." When someone else urged him to "stay safe and take a small concealed club," he responded that he would "have something with me."

McAbee was still a sheriff's deputy in Williamson County, Tennessee. He showed up in a black tactical uniform, "SHERIFF" inscribed on his vest, and a patch to show his allegiance to an anti-government militia organization called the Three Percenters. McAbee was an anti-government sheriff's deputy on the government payroll. He wasn't at work on January 6th because he told his bosses he needed time to recuperate from a car crash. But he wasn't so injured that he couldn't come to the Capitol to attack police officers. McAbee is one of those law enforcement officers who didn't deserve to wear the badge. Prior to his time with Williamson County, he was employed by Knox County Sheriff's Office, and before that, the Cherokee County Sheriff's Office in Georgia. While at the sheriff's office in Georgia, he was disciplined for taunting inmates with pepper spray and lying to them about their release dates. An officer with problems.

Barnhart's credentials were that when he was eighteen, he was sentenced in connection with a riot on the Michigan State University campus in East Lansing. He helped tip over a car. He was charged with a felony, punishable by up to five years in prison. He was a kid, so he was sentenced to forty-five days in jail for unlawful assembly for a riot.

Whitton, a fencing contractor, was heard shouting on video to police officers on January 6th, "You're gonna die tonight." But I'm getting ahead of myself.

At approximately 4:20 p.m., Metropolitan Police officers assumed a post in an archway at the access point of the

US Capitol's lower western terrace. Among the MPD officers at that post were Officer A. W., Officer B. M., and Officer C. M. Shortly after assuming the post, all three officers were brutally assaulted by rioters who were part of a mob that had gathered outside of the US Capitol. Officer A. W. sustained a laceration to the head that required staples to close, and Officer B. M. sustained an abrasion to his nose and right cheek and minor bruising to his left shoulder.

As the officers assembled on the west side of the Capitol, one was knocked to the ground. Sabol climbed up the stairs where the officer was lying and yanked his baton out of his hand. Mullins then grabbed the officer and pulled him farther down the stairs and into the crowd. At the same time, Whitton began beating another officer with a crutch and then Whitton and Barnhart pulled the officer by his head and helmet down the stairs over the top of the first officer. Courson, who was at the bottom of the stairs, started beating the officer with a baton.

Sabol then ran back up the stairs and used the baton he had stolen from one officer to press against the neck of the second officer. Sabol and the others dragged that officer farther into the crowd and continued beating him. They ripped off his helmet, maced him, took his gas mask and MPD-issued cell phone, and kicked and stomped him. Then Stager beat the second officer with a flagpole. Courson beat him with a baton. Barnhart pushed other rioters from behind, into the line of officers, then approached the officers and struck at them with the base of a flagpole. Whitton walked up to the line of officers in the archway and kicked at them, struck a riot shield held by an MPD officer, and shouted, "You're gonna die tonight."

When the rioters did get into the Capitol, what did they do? They destroyed offices. They intentionally knocked over bookshelves, filing cabinets, tables, and chairs. They broke windows. They splintered doors. They sprayed tear gas and bear spray on paintings. They shit and urinated on the floors. All in all, they did more than $2 million in damage. I guess the floors and doors and walls were somehow complicit in stealing the election from Trump.

And when it was over and their master, Donald Trump, patted them on their heads and told them to go home, the insurrectionists wimped away and hid like cowards. They didn't "stop the steal." They didn't protect democracy. If anything, they weakened it.

For all the talk, for all the bluster, for all the lies, for all the plans, they traveled to the nation's Capitol from hundreds of miles away and left without accomplishing anything—except brutality, destruction, and death.

7

RACISTS, QANON,
CRIMINALS ≠ PATRIOTS

in·sur·rec·tion/ ˌinsəˈrekSH(ə)n/noun **A violent upris-
ing against an authority or government**
in·sur·rec·tion·ist/ insə-ˈrek-sh(ə-)nist /noun **A person
who provokes or takes part in an insurrection**

When I turn on the radio or television or go on the
internet or social media and hear the insurrectionists
who stormed the Capitol described as patriots, as heroes,
it makes me sick, fucking sick to my stomach. I want to
throw up. I want to slap the hell out of somebody. The
insurrectionists who invaded the Capitol were not patriots. They were terrorists. They incited fear, and that's
what they wanted to do. They tried to overturn the will
of the American people.

They are criminals. If they weren't before, they are
now, which is why hundreds of them have been arrested

and convicted or pled guilty. I did what I could to send some of the worst domestic terrorists to prison when I testified at the first Oath Keepers trial. The Oath Keepers were one of the few really organized groups at the riot. They came to the Capitol in riot gear. They brought weapons. They had planned for months how they would overthrow the government. So, they were charged with one of the most serious charges the Department of Justice brought against the rioters, seditious conspiracy, a technical term for treason.

I have to admit, the trial was a nerve-racking event. I was anxious, but not because I was nervous about what I would say. I was prepared. I had gone over my testimony for three days with the prosecuting attorney for the Justice Department. My lawyer, David Laufman, was there during the preparation. He is a former prosecutor for the Justice Department. The Justice Department attorney helped me tell my story. "Don't talk about things you have not been asked." "Be clear and concise." "Tell the truth; tell the truth; tell the truth. A good witness is truthful and consistent."

She's right. You can't go on the stand and flip flop. Your story can't change every time you tell it. I know what happened. I know my story. My question for the prosecutor was what should I expect from the defense attorney. The defense, she said, is going to try to defame your credibility or suggest that you are, or were, stressed out and may have misremembered something. I get anxious because a lot of people, not just me and the other officers, want justice. People want these jokers to pay for what they did to our country. So, me testifying is a continuance of my public service. I owed it to my country to testify.

On the morning of the trial, October 31, 2022, the Justice Department sent a car to pick up me and my lawyer at 8 a.m. from my lawyer's office. There were two FBI agents in the car. Outside the courtroom, there were media everywhere. The FBI took me in through a back entrance and handed me off to the US Marshals. They knew I was coming because the court posts the witness list the day before. I went into the witness holding room and waited before I was to testify. The room is right outside the courtroom. It's a chair, a table, and four walls. It's not fancy at all. It's probably the size of a walk-in closet.

For the occasion, I wore my Capitol Police officer's dress uniform. While I waited, I got a visit from the specialists at the Howard C. Liebengood Center for Wellness. The center helps officers relax before their testimony. It has been there for a while as part of our peer support team, but it was named for one of the Capitol Police officers who died by suicide in the wake of January 6th. The center sent more than one person over and even brought the support dogs for other federal officers who were testifying in court that day. I did some breathing exercises. They helped center me and helped me relax. I was ready to testify. I went to the witness stand.

The prosecuting attorney began by asking me a series of questions. Some of it was to establish my credibility and to get me used to the environment.

Prosecuting Attorney: Do you recall hearing shots fired over the radio that day?

Me: I do.

Prosecuting Attorney: And in a chaotic day, why do you remember hearing shots fired? Why does that stick out to you?

Me: It's the potential for loss of life. And that's the most important thing, what we're—that's our job. We're there to protect life.

Prosecuting Attorney: And when you interacted with these individuals in the Crypt, was it before or after the shots fired?

Me: It was after the shots have fired. I heard the call for shots fired, and that's why I responded up the stairwell.

Prosecuting Attorney: And how soon after shots fired did you interact with those people in the Crypt?

Me: A minute or so.

Prosecuting Attorney: Now, I want to ask you about this interaction in the Crypt. What do you remember saying to these individuals?

Me: "Get out." There was a lady that asked where the bathroom was. "Where's the exit?" "The same way you came in." The individuals that offered to stand in front of me, I told them that there were officers getting the shit kicked out of them, and there were officers down and officers hurt. And, again, like I said in the other video, "Y'all are fucking us up."

Prosecuting Attorney: And what did they say after you said there were officers injured? What did these individuals in the Crypt say to you?

Me: They appeared taken back, almost like humanized for a minute. And that's when they offered to stand there to keep anybody else from going down to the lower west terrace area where officers were incapacitated.

Prosecuting Attorney: And what did you say in response?

Me: I thought about it. I don't need your help. That's what I thought. F y'all. But I ended up allowing them to stand there. I took two steps, three steps down to create distance and allowed time for other officers to come.

Prosecuting Attorney: And how many of these individuals who stood in front of you, how many were there?

Me: About three, maybe four.

Prosecuting Attorney: Now, Officer Dunn, in the previous video that we observed, did anyone in that video offer to assist you?

Me: No.

Prosecuting Attorney: Did this individual, at this point in time, offer to assist you?

Me: No.

Prosecuting Attorney: This individual on the right?

Me: No.

It's the job of the defense attorney to throw some shade on your story. So, they suggest things, like maybe your memory is faulty or maybe the situation wasn't as tense as you've made it sound. That's what the Oath Keepers' different attorneys tried to do.

Defense Attorney: So, in this photo, you're by yourself; is that fair to say?

Me: Yes.

Defense Attorney: And your rifle is down, you're not holding it, correct?

Me: It's slung around my body.

Defense Attorney: Right. And your arms are at your sides, like you're not reaching for your gun, right?

Me: Correct.

Defense Attorney: And you're not reaching for any other type of weapon that may be on you?

Me: No, that's correct.

Defense Attorney: In fact, you appear kind of almost relaxed, like you're not in an offensive posture; fair to say?

Me: No, that's not fair to say. I was not relaxed at any point during that day.

Their lawyer suggested that after members of the Oath Keepers invaded the Capitol, they tried to help me control other rioters and insurrectionists. That was bullshit, and they knew it. So, when the prosecutor asked me if they were trying to help me, I quickly responded, "They were trying to get past me, and I stopped them. They didn't. I did."

Elmer Stewart Rhodes III, the founder and leader of the Oath Keepers, and Kelly Meggs, the leader of the Florida chapter, were found guilty of the most serious charges. Rhodes was sentenced to eighteen years in prison. Meggs was sentenced to twelve years. I am proud to have been a part of helping convict those traitors and send them to prison, where they belong. The fact that Rhodes and other Oath Keepers will be spending years behind bars doesn't make me happy. What would make me happy is if none of this had ever happened.

Four more Oath Keepers were convicted of seditious conspiracy early in 2023 at the second trial. Prosecutors didn't need my testimony for that trial, but when they called me to testify for the third trial of those bastards, I was more than happy to help. So, I prepped again, and in March 2023, I testified at the third trial.

The Justice Department prosecutors asked me to offer an impact statement for the judge to consider at sentencing. Here is part of what I wrote:

> I stand here today as a victim of the defendants'
> actions on January 6. But my pain didn't end on
> that day. Because I have told the truth about what
> happened, I have had to install security cameras
> around my home. I live in constant fear for my
> daughter, my loved ones, and myself. My dad feels
> it's necessary to tell me to be careful every time we
> talk on the phone. "Keep your head on a swivel,"
> he says. When I am out attempting to live a regular
> life, whether that be at a restaurant, at the mall, or
> even at work, I am always hyper-vigilant about my
> surroundings. I have been a police officer for
> fifteen years, so I have always paid attention to my
> surroundings, but now it's different. Instead of
> worrying and paying attention for the well-being
> of others, I now worry about my own safety and
> well-being. Whenever I see someone in cargo

pants or anything that looks remotely close to
tactical gear, I wonder if they were a part of the
insurrection. I get anxious, I start to clinch my
teeth, I notice a rise in my heart rate, and I look for
the closest place to retreat to for peace of mind. Of
course, at my workplace—the US Capitol—there
is no such place to which I can retreat. Because of
the defendants' actions on January 6, every day at
work in the Capitol building evokes in me the
feeling that I am at a never-ending crime scene,
rather than the citadel of American democracy. As
I walk through the halls of Congress every day, I'm
reminded of terrible things that I saw, that I
experienced, or that one of my fellow officers told
me happened in the place we are standing in. I
used to enjoy coming to work each day, proud to
be a police officer. But the defendants ripped that
all away from me.

Even after all this time, giving that statement was
extremely hard for me. I had practiced my speech one
hundred times, but inside the courtroom, it was different.
The two officers who read their statements before me
began crying, and I could feel my emotions bubbling up.
As I spoke, I noticed I started getting angry. I dug my
nails into the podium as I continued. After I finished, I
quickly left the courtroom to compose myself.

I am still amazed that after everything, some people are still trying to protect those traitors. It's disgusting. They honor them on their websites and through social media. They call them "real Americans." Even worse are the elected officials in state after state who act like the horror of the insurrection was a small thing, particularly because so many of my fellow officers shed blood protecting our nation. That day brought out the worst of America—racists, conspiracy wackos, and convicted felons.

The air was saturated with bigotry long before the violence took place. Among the sea of humanity that descended on the Capitol that day were thousands of white supremacists and anti-Semites. They displayed various symbols of hate. The most visible were the Confederate flags. The Confederate flag is so universally recognized as a symbol of hate and racism that the US military will not allow it in any form on any of its bases—not as a flag, not as a bumper sticker, not as patches, not as a T-shirt. Many of the people who support that shit use the excuse that it's part of our history.

The Ku Klux Klan, the White Citizens Council, and other racist organizations used the flag to terrorize Black people and Jews throughout the country, not just in the south but also in rallies from Washington State to Washington, DC. The same groups waved them as they murdered Black people and Jews across America to ensure segregation and subjugation would continue to exist.

In one of the most horrific recent episodes, Dylann Roof took photographs with the Confederate flag before he murdered nine members of the Emanuel African Methodist Episcopal Church in 2015 during a prayer service. He said he hoped killing those Black worshippers would start a race war. His allegiance to the Confederate flag caused then South Carolina governor Nikki Haley to recognize it as a symbol of white supremacy and hate. She had it removed from all state buildings, where it had flown for years.

I already told you about my racist encounter with a bunch of Trump supporters that day. As I told the January 6th Committee when I testified, I was called a nigger as I was protecting a corridor and giving time for House Speaker Nancy Pelosi's staff to escape to safety. It was first uttered by a woman in a pink MAGA shirt.

"Hey, this nigger voted for Biden," she said.

Then about twenty of them chimed in, "Boo! Fucking nigger."

Many of my Black Capitol police colleagues had stories like mine. They just didn't want to come forward like I did, and I understand why. One fellow officer said a group that had gotten inside the Capitol told him, "Put your gun down, and we'll show you what kind of nigger you really are!" The irony of that moment was that more than seventy years after Sergeant Isaac Woodard—after the civil rights movement; after the deaths of Emmett

Till, Medgar Evers, Martin Luther King, and others; after the Supreme Court declared segregation unconstitutional; after Black people's continued service in every war; and after the election of an African American as president of the United States—we were just "niggers" to them, just like that Black veteran of World War II who had come home from war only to be beaten and blinded by white cops.

Just like him, we were wearing our uniforms and badges, signifying our service to our nation. But just like Woodard, to them, we were throw-away people to be despised, hated, and derided, not because of something we had done, but merely because of the color of our skin.

And all that Stop the Steal bullshit was just that, bullshit. January 6th was never about politics. It wasn't about election fraud. That was an excuse for people to do some shit they had wanted to do in the first place. Those people came to the Capitol based on something they wanted to believe. Trump didn't brainwash them. If anything, they brainwashed themselves. They wanted to believe that. They chose to believe that nonsense. They are like the people who seek second, third, and then fourth opinions until they finally hear the one they want to hear. Then they go with that lie.

It is not that the truth wasn't out there. William Barr, the attorney general who had always backed Trump, said publicly that the US Justice Department looked for corruption in the election, at Trump's request, and it did not find any. Not one person in charge of state elections in any of the fifty states could find any evidence of cheating against Trump, including in states like Georgia, where Republicans were in charge and oversaw the process.

State and federal judges threw out more than fifty legal challenges by Trump's lawyers. Not only that, but Republicans also picked up fifteen seats in the House of Representatives in the 2020 election by beating the Democrats in eleven states. So, were they saying the election machines worked for those Republicans but not for Trump?

What's worse, Trump knew it was not true, and he continues to tell the lie. His own campaign paid more than $600,000 for Berkeley Research Group to look into the election, and they told him that the claims of dead voters and bad machines were not true. He hired a second firm and paid them $750,000, and they told him the same thing. People he hired told him his claims were a lie. It never happened.

Like I said, the insurrectionists came to the Capitol based on a lie they wanted to believe, and many lies they already believed.

What gave them so much traction is that, these days, the crazies keep finding each other on the internet. The Pizzagate nuts, the QAnon wackos, the Alex Jones idiots. They had their little Q signs and emblems pinned on their clothes on January 6th. We saw them. This stuff is so insane, it's hard for me to believe anybody takes it seriously, but they do.

It's hard for me to believe that this madness existed in the first place and that it has been around as long as it has. It started in 2016 with Pizzagate. I wasn't paying attention to it that far back, and I really didn't know anything about it until there was a shooting not far from where I live. Apparently, beginning in October 2016, just before the presidential election, right-wing nuts began writing on Facebook and Twitter that Hillary Clinton and the Democrats were kidnapping children and holding them as sex slaves at pizza places around the nation, including one in northwest DC.

When a guy named Edgar Welch in Salisbury, North Carolina, heard about it, he spent three days watching videos and reading about it on the internet. Welch was twenty-eight at the time. He then decided he needed to investigate the matter himself. So, this dude concocted a plan and tried to get some friends to join him. He told his friends that he believed it would involve "sacrificing the lives of a few for the lives of many." One of his friends told him to stay home and do some more research, but Welch was ready to go.

So, on Sunday, December 4, Welch left his home and his two children in Salisbury and drove six hours to "rescue" the children the crazy people on the internet said were being held in DC. He even videotaped himself driving up. He arrived at the Comet Ping Pong restaurant at around three in the afternoon. Inside his car was a 9-mm

AR-15 assault rifle loaded with approximately thirty bullets, a fully loaded .38-caliber revolver, and a loaded shotgun with extra shotgun shells. I saw a photo of him on the news afterward. He was a slim guy with sandy blond hair. He had on a T-shirt and faded jeans. He wasn't dressed like one of those wannabe warriors, all decked out in camo like some of the idiots we were looking at on January 6th.

Welch parked and then marched inside the restaurant. It was a normal day, so customers with their children were milling around inside. Welch was carrying an assault rifle and the pistol. Frightened patrons bolted out the doors with their children. Employees ran out too. Welch came to a locked door, which he tried to open with a butter knife to check for kidnapped children. When that did not work, he shot the door several times. After about twenty minutes, Welch left the building, apparently to wait outside for the police. When they arrived, he surrendered peacefully. He told the police he did so because he didn't find "children were being harbored in the restaurant."

Stay with me, because this is going to tell you a lot about January 6th and what I said about people believing what they want to believe. Welch pled guilty. He got four years in prison. Think about it. He spent three days looking at bullshit on the internet, and now he was going to prison for four years. He admitted he was wrong, and he told the judge he had no reason to believe what he believed or do what he did. He said there were no children being kept hostage in the building. He was wrong, and he realized his lunacy.

You might think this foolishness would have ended there, but it didn't. When the people promoting this conspiracy on the internet heard about his confession, they said that Welch was a "crisis actor." The incident was a "false flag." All of it had been made up to throw people like them off the trail while the abuse of children kidnapped by Hillary Clinton and the Democrats continued in pizza places across America.

Edgar Welch was going to jail for four years because he believed in a lie spun by idiots that sucked in other gullible people. His children would be without their father for those years, without his love, without his guidance, without his financial and moral support. And the people who concocted this madness just continued with their lies and stupidity and dismissed Edgar Welch because he didn't fit into the lies they kept telling. He never happened. They continued to believe what they wanted to believe, just like the people at the Capitol on January 6th did.

So, the theory kept growing, only it got even crazier. It expanded into what we now know as QAnon, a wacky, anti-Semitic theory about a worldwide organization of Jewish, Satan-worshipping child abusers, Democrats, actors, and elites—President Biden, Barack Obama,

George Soros, Oprah Winfrey, Tom Hanks, Ellen DeGe-
neres, Pope Francis, the Dalai Lama, and others—who
were not only abusing children but also drinking the
children's blood so they could stay young. Oh yeah, and
Donald Trump and other government insiders were
secretly fighting against them and would bring the bad
guys to justice.

It spread like wildfire on Twitter, Facebook, and You-
Tube, until it had millions of followers. By the time
Welch got out of prison in May 2020, it was everywhere.
In fact, there were thirty-six people running for Congress
that year who swore by it. Two of them were elected.
What's so sick is that one of the QAnon "influencers"
who the followers tuned in to, a man who called President Biden a pedophile, was, in fact, a pedophile. David
Todeschini, a registered sex offender and QAnon propo-
gandist, served five years in prison for the sexual abuse of
an eight-year-old boy.

Ashli Babbitt, unfortunately, believed the conspiracy
theories and Donald Trump. Babbitt was shot by a Capitol Police officer when she defied an order and tried to
climb through a window at the Capitol. Babbitt was an
Air Force veteran, like my father. She served tours in Iraq
and Afghanistan. Six of her years in service were with the
Capital Guardians unit of the District of Columbia Air
National Guard. Its mission is to defend DC and stop
any civil unrest.

I commend Babbitt for her service, but somewhere along the way, things with her went wrong, and she began a downward spiral. Some of her issues surfaced when she was in the military. She was demoted three times.

In 2016, she faced criminal charges of reckless endangerment in Maryland. She rear-ended the car of the girlfriend of the man with whom she was having an affair. Babbitt was married to her first husband, Timothy McEntee, when she began an affair with Aaron Babbitt. Aaron Babbitt was living with his girlfriend, Celeste Norris. They had been together for six years.

When Norris found out about the affair, she moved out and told McEntee that his wife was cheating. Months later, Babbitt, then still named McEntee, spotted Norris's car waiting at a stop sign in Frederick, Maryland. She made a U-turn, chased Norris's car down, and began repeatedly smashing her SUV into it. When Norris pulled over to the side of the road after calling police, Babbitt came to her window and threatened to beat her up. Norris asked for, and received, a restraining order against Babbitt because, she said, she was afraid of her. After continued harassment, Norris received a second restraining order in 2017.

Babbitt divorced her first husband and moved with her new one to San Diego, her hometown. By the time she showed up at the Capitol, she had leaned into all the Trump election lies and QAnon conspiracy theories.

Beginning in 2016, she used her Twitter account to praise Trump, denigrate undocumented immigrants, and express support for the extremist QAnon. Even before Trump's election, she wrote to him, "#love" beside his name and above a photo of three signs nailed to a tree: "Make America Great Again," "H FOR PRISON," and "CHRISTIAN DEPLORABLES LIVE HERE." On Election Day, she wrote to Trump, "Today we save America from the tyranny, collusion and corruption."

On January 6th, she messaged that it was up to people like her to reinstate Trump to stop the Satan-worshipping, kidnapping, blood-drinking elites.

"Nothing can stop us . . . they can try and try but the storm is here and it is descending upon DC in less than 24 hours . . . dark to light," she wrote. These days, Babbitt is being portrayed as a hero. Trump wrote on Truth Social, his social media platform, "ASHLI BABBITT WAS MURDERED!!!" Trump praised her in one of his speeches and, in a rebuke to a member of Congress who said the officer who shot her did his job, Trump wrote about the officer who "shot and killed Great Patriot Ashli Babbitt."

She has been called a "freedom fighter" and the "first victim of the second Civil War" by right-wing websites and activists. One person wrote, "The beautiful young woman who was executed will be remembered as a martyr." So, on January 6th, we were facing a sea of racists, self-deluded people like Babbitt, and a bunch of idiots who just wanted to fight. But also—and here's the truth about who was at the Capitol on January 6th that the media and most people don't talk about—a lot of the people outside the Capitol that day were just plain criminals long before that day ever happened. I'm talking about thieves and con artists with felony convictions.

Let's start with Enrique Tarrio, the leader of the Proud Boys. If you recall, the Proud Boys were the group Trump told to "stand back and stand by" during the presidential debate when he was asked to publicly reject white supremacist groups like them and the Oath Keepers. They were one of three militia groups that played a large role in the Capitol riot.

Now, Enrique and three of his boys are behind bars after being convicted of seditious conspiracy for their part in the attack on the Capitol. It took a week, but the jury found him and his friends guilty of thirty-one of forty-six counts. The jury's verdict makes Tarrio a three-time convicted felon.

Tarrio began his criminal career in 2004 in Miami, when he stole a $55,000 motorcycle and tried to resell it. He pled guilty to two felonies, but because it was his first offense and he was young, he was sentenced to three years' probation and community service. Real criminals like Tarrio, however, don't take a second chance and get on with their lives. They keep lying and thieving.

Tarrio was convicted of four more felonies a few years later. He and his accomplice were caught after stealing $1.2 million in diabetes test strips from a laboratory and reselling them. This was in 2012. Tarrio was sentenced to three years in prison, but he cut a deal with federal prosecutors to provide evidence against his friends so that they would be convicted and he would receive a reduced sentence. So, after rolling over on thirteen other criminals, he was released in December 2014 after sixteen months with two years' probation and ordered to pay restitution for the full $1.2 million. To protect his street cred, Tarrio lies whenever he is asked about being a government informant, but the records are there.

Tarrio also pled guilty in 2021 to the destruction of property, which was a Black Lives Matter flag, and a reduced charge of attempting to possess a high-capacity ammunition feeding device and was sentenced to five months in prison. Patriot?

Let me run down the list of a few more criminals at the Capitol on January 6th.

Kash Lee Kelly was sentenced to sixty days in November 2022 for his participation in the riot. But by then, he had been in prison for a year for drug dealing. Kelly had already been convicted when he joined the other insurrectionists in DC. He was just waiting to hear how much time he would spend behind bars. One month after he left DC, Kelly was sentenced to four years in prison and three years' probation for trafficking cocaine and marijuana in Indiana.

Peter J. Schwartz was sentenced in 2019 to five years in prison on weapons charges and for terrorizing local residents. Schwartz has a long criminal history. He was only forty-nine, but federal prosecutors say he has had nearly forty prior convictions over more than thirty years for crimes such as assault or threatening officers. Schwartz was at the Capitol because the prison officials released him and others to protect them from COVID-19, which, without a vaccine, certainly might have killed him. Instead of staying at home and going to work in Uniontown, Pennsylvania, he and his wife, Shelly Stallings, decided to come to the Capitol to fight us.

That day, a man next to Schwartz grabbed a bag of pepper spray from a Capitol Police officer and handed some of the containers to Schwartz. He immediately handed one to his wife and told her to spray the officers in the face. All three immediately began spraying the officers' eyes, even as officers tried to turn away. Schwartz also hit an officer with a chair. This is what Schwartz posted on Facebook the day after the attack: "What happened yesterday was the opening of a war. I was there, and whether people will acknowledge it or not, we are now at war." Schwartz's wife pled guilty to seven federal charges. A defiant Schwartz went to trial and was convicted of four felonies, including assaulting, resisting, or impeding law enforcement officers using a dangerous weapon and interfering with a law enforcement officer. He was sentenced in May to fourteen years in prison, the longest sentence handed out so far for any of the people who invaded the Capitol.

James McGrew, an ex-Marine and QAnon follower, was still on parole for several crimes when he assaulted two police officers at the Capitol. He fled DC and then led FBI agents on a chase from his home in Carlsbad, California, to Mexico to Glendale, Arizona, where he was arrested. FBI identified him from a booking photo in 2012 that showed a huge "King James" tattoo across his stomach. McGrew had been in and out of jail since he left the service in 2008 for multiple thefts in Mississippi, primarily to pay for his drug addiction. By the way, parole is temporary release before the completion of a sentence on the promise of good behavior.

McGrew pled guilty for his January 6th offenses and admitted that he was the person who shouted "Let's go" fourteen times before pushing barricades into the police to get into the Capitol. Once inside, McGrew struck a DC police officer who was trying to move rioters out of the Great Rotunda and later struck another officer and lunged for his baton. In another scuffle with another officer, he successfully snatched a baton. About forty-five minutes later, as McGrew was near the Lower West Tunnel entrance, someone in the crowd handed him a detached wooden handrail with the metal brackets still affixed to it. He launched the nearly six-foot piece over his head toward officers in the tunnel, according to the plea. It appeared to strike an officer's visor or shield.

Kene Brian Lazo, forty-four, came to the Capitol decked out in a helmet, goggles, and other tactical gear, with an American flag draped around his shoulders. Lazo was recorded running around the Capitol chanting, "Our house!" He pled guilty to demonstrating, parading, and picketing in the Capitol building, a misdemeanor. But Lazo had much bigger issues ahead of him. Six months after January 6th, he was arrested on separate charges for contributing to the delinquency of a child under age thirteen; aggravated sexual battery of a child under thirteen; intercourse by force, threat, or intimidation; forcible sodomy by force, threat, or of an incapacitated or physically helpless person over the age of thirteen; and two counts of simple assault. Lazo pled guilty in two separate cases to two counts of assault against a family member. In each case, he was sentenced to twelve months' incarceration, with eleven months suspended. His sentence included two years of "uniform good behavior"—in other words, no arrests during that time—and substance abuse counseling, and he is to have no contact with the victim. The sexual crimes were not dropped. Instead, they have been held in abeyance as part of the plea agreement.

Jia Liu, twenty-six, was arrested after January 6th and pled guilty in October 2022 for entering the Capitol with the other insurrectionists. But before he could be convicted, Liu was arrested for a different crime. He was arrested in February of the same year with an accomplice for distributing vaccine cards to at least three hundred people who had not gotten vaccinated but who wanted proof that they had. The way the scheme worked was that Steven Rodriguez, a nurse, saw patients who came to the clinic for vaccination appointments but didn't actually get shots. Rodriguez allegedly wasted doses of the lifesaving treatment by disposing of their doses of the vaccine. They are also accused of making more than seventy false entries in immunization databases.

Shane Woods was one of those people I told you about who came to the Capitol to pick a fight. He is also one of at least two January 6th rioters who were charged a year later in separate incidents with killing people while driving drunk. The other is Emily Hernandez. You may have spotted Hernandez in the photo in which she is standing inside the Capitol, just steps away from the idiot wearing the "Camp Auschwitz" sweatshirt. She was grinning widely, proud of herself, as she held a piece of the nameplate that belonged to Nancy Pelosi.

Woods killed Lauren Wegner of Skokie, Illinois, when he crashed head-on into her car in November 2022. He was driving northbound in the southbound lanes on

Interstate 55 in Sagamon County. His blood alcohol level was 1.77, more than twice the legal limit in Illinois. He was fleeing a cop after being pulled over.

Just a month earlier, he pled guilty to felony assault of a law enforcement officer and a member of the media at the Capitol on January 6th. As a Capitol Police officer was pursuing a man who pepper sprayed her, Woods lowered his shoulder and rammed into her, sending her flying through the air and into a downed bicycle barricade. That was at about 2:10 p.m. Woods wasn't finished brutalizing people. At around 5 p.m., he joined a bunch of rioters who were destroying the media's video cameras and other equipment outside the Capitol. When Woods saw a reporter walking away with his video camera, he took a running start and hit the man with a blindside shoulder tackle, knocking him to the ground. The reporter fell and dropped the camera.

Hernandez, who lived in Sullivan, Missouri, was driving drunk and the wrong way on Interstate 44 on January 5, 2022, when her car struck the vehicle of Victoria Wilson head-on. Wilson was thirty-two and lived with her husband in St. Clair, Missouri. Wilson died, and her husband was injured. Five days after the fatal crash, Hernandez, then twenty-two, pled guilty to a misdemeanor trespassing charge at the Capitol. She was sentenced to thirty days in jail. Two more heroes?

These people shouldn't be called patriots, nor should we feel sorry for them. They didn't care about me or my coworkers. They damn sure didn't care about the rest of America. They were self-centered and self-serving. They were hateful, deluded, and violent. The words *hero* or *patriot* should never be applied to them

Let me tell you about a real hero, a real patriot. Her name is Christine. She is thirty-two years old and in her sixth year as a Capitol Police officer. Christine is five feet two and weighs 135 pounds. There's nothing big about Christine—except her heart and her will and her integrity and her commitment. I'm six feet seven, and Christine is one of the people I look *up* to.

Christine comes from a military family. Her father served in the US Air Force and later in the Army National Guard. Her brother did six years in the Air National Guard, and her sister is still a member of the Air National Guard. And her grandmother? Her grandmother was a US Marine. So, Christine knows a little something about service to her country. Before joining the Capitol Police, she had worked a few jobs as a sales associate for various retail operations. Until January 6th, she thought she may have found her calling.

Christine works with me on the First Responder Unit. Her collateral assignment on January 6th was with the Civil Disturbance Unit, which, as mentioned earlier, is the heavily armored unit whose job is to control violent crowds. Like all of us, Christine reported early on January 6th, around six o'clock in the morning, and immediately headed for her Civil Disturbance Unit platoon. The unit is made up of several platoons. Each platoon is about forty people. As she and her fellow officers prepared to put on all their gear on the day of the insurrection, her platoon commander told the unit something Christine had never heard before. They were told not to put on their protective armor. Instead, they were to take their armor to a nearby bus and leave it there. If they needed it, they would sprint from their position to the bus, take about ten minutes to put on their gear, and then go back to the action and quell the violence.

Let that sink in for a minute.

Tens of thousands of people who had been invited to the Capitol by the president with a tweet that read "Will be wild" were gathering outside, and the unit that is trained and geared to quell violence was told to *not* be prepared. They were told to *not* put on the special equipment they use to do their job.

Give it another minute.

Just like it doesn't make any sense to you, it didn't make any sense to Christine or her team, and it doesn't make any sense to me. When her unit questioned the platoon commander, the commander said those were the orders passed down by leadership higher up.

Christine and her unit were assigned to the west side of the Capitol, which is where the biggest crowd was. When they got there, they could see the bus below, but the crowd was already between them and the bus. There was no way they could have even made it to the bus for their armor from where they were. To make matters worse, the bus took off a few minutes later, because the driver didn't want to get overwhelmed by the crowd.

No bus. No gear. No nothing.

At around 12:40 p.m., the crowd hopped the barriers. For Christine, it was a frightening moment. "When they finally breached that line, I felt an immediate gut punch," she told me. "Through all of the demonstrations, they stayed on their side of the barriers, and we stayed on our side. I was just so used to them staying on their side, and us on ours. It was shocking. Even during the George Floyd protests, they stayed on their side, and we stayed on ours. Even when we had to go into the crowd, they let us do our police work in peace. They didn't attack us. We didn't attack them. There was no beating on officers."

From then on, it was just madness. Christine and the other officers were in hand-to-hand combat. Insurrectionists doused them with WD-40 and bear spray. They pelted them with batteries, beer cans, soup cans, and rocks. They tore away parts of the staging for the upcoming presidential inauguration and used it to beat the officers. Christine told me that the spray on her jacket became so thick that it was reactivating in her face, so she stripped down in the biting cold to her vest and a long-sleeved shirt.

Ultimately, she found some cases of water about thirty feet from where the action was. She flushed her eyes and went back into the fight. And that, she said, was exactly what it was—a fight.

"Those people were just looking for a fight," she told me. She repeatedly retreated to flush her eyes and then got back into the fight. One of her friends on the force was hit square in the face. He collapsed. The other officers took him to the Rayburn Building, where doctors and medics could treat him.

Christine told me she was preparing to go back outside, but some DC police officers rerouted her inside to help them chase down rioters who had gotten into the building. She said she was like a pinball, bouncing from one crisis to the next. She was on the first floor, in the basement, in the Rotunda, and around the House chamber. She reminded me of something that so many people have forgotten: in addition to protecting the members of Congress, we had to protect the workers in the Capitol—the cleaning staff, the mason workers, the groundskeepers, the electrical staff, and the restaurant workers.

There was more hitting, more kicking. She'd grab hold of one rioter, and he would weasel away, and she and the other officers would chase down another. At one point, she took a heavy blow to the face. She knew it was bad when she got hit, but she said she couldn't stop. She said she didn't feel pain until around eight o'clock that night. When the swelling kicked in, her superiors had her transported by ambulance to the Washington Hospital Center. There was a lot of swelling and a lot of pain, she told me, but, thankfully, the doctors found nothing was broken.

Other officers were being treated at the hospital. Christine was released from the hospital at midnight. She came back to the Capitol. I asked her why she didn't go home. She said, "I wanted to go back to work because I wanted to make sure my friends were all right."

We lost Christine that night—not to death or injury but to the same feelings of betrayal that so many of us feel. She describes it as "a resigned bitterness." I understand, because I feel the same way. We were let down. We were let down by our citizens, by our elected officials, and by our leadership within the Capitol Police.

Two years later, we are still waiting for answers, still waiting for vindication—still waiting to be made whole.

8

FINDING MY WAY BACK FROM THEIR INSANITY

Almost immediately after January 6th, it got dark for me, mentally and emotionally. I mean really dark. I struggled every workday morning—from the moment the alarm clock rang to when I got dressed and headed out of my house and into the slowly awakening city. A mix of anger and depression would immediately stir inside me and intensify as I stepped out the door and slipped behind the wheel of my Harley-Davidson Ford F-150.

Even now it's there, but to a lesser degree. As usual, I nose the truck off my street and onto Georgia Avenue, past the familiar sights—the 7-Eleven where I buy lottery tickets, the Subway, the Brazilian Boutique, the apartment buildings. I turn left at Target and glide by a foreign-car repair shop and then the Kentucky Fried Chicken/Taco Bell as I roll down Blair Road. It becomes

North Capitol Street, which leads straight into work. The blues rides along with me. My blues comes with a hip-hop beat. My phone is always Bluetoothed to the truck, so I search for a track to fortify me for the day. Maybe Jay-Z. Maybe Tupac, "Me Against the World."

[Slap! Boom. Boom.]
[Slap! Boom. Boom.]

When will I finally get to rest through this oppression?
They punish the people that's askin' questions

I push down the anger and hurt, which, by now, I can almost feel crawling up my throat. I vow to make this a good day. I'm still rolling toward the place where I don't want to go. Before January 6th, I was a guy who was always early for work. I looked forward to my job. I looked forward to chatting up other Capitol Police officers during roll call. After getting my assignment, I happily met and talked with some of the thousands of people who come to the Capitol every day. After the insurrection, I became a guy who was late all the time, just a minute or two, and I was no longer the bubbly person who wanted to be there to provide a place for Americans to enjoy and practice their democracy. I just didn't give a damn.

Finally, I arrive at work. I park. Now, I try to find the emotional strength to walk into the Capitol. In those early days, it was hard, real hard. I didn't want to go into the building. Early on, every day at work I would replay January 6th. When I walked down the halls or past certain parts of the building, I relived what happened in that space. I could hear the voices and the shouting. I could smell the odors. I'm replaying that day on a loop and wondering what I could have done differently. I get angry all over again. I'm thinking, "I can't let these fuckers get away with that shit. I'm not shutting up about this shit, ever."

I remember how in those early days after the insurrection, I felt terribly alone. I didn't want to talk to anybody, and I really didn't want anybody to talk to me. I still feel alone, but not as much. But when I have a thought, I still struggle to think of someone I can share it with. So, I often just keep it to myself.

One of the amazing things that happened after January 6th was all the support we got from our brother and sister law enforcement officers. I mean, the next day, they started showing up from all over the nation: US Marshals from Texas, the Prince George's County Police Department, Alexandria Police. It went on like that for months. The New York Police, the Atlanta Police. Cops from all over. They stayed three or four days and then another group came. They came there to be with us, so we could have someone to talk with if we needed it.

Unfortunately, I wasn't really ready to open up and talk to other officers, at least not like that. I didn't share too much. I'd be on post, and an officer from another police force would stop by to make small talk. We would talk for a minute, but I wasn't really feeling it. It could lead to some awkward moments. We'd just be standing there. He's there; I'm there; and we're not talking to each other. People have got to be ready for something like that. For me, it was awkward.

"So, how are you doing?"

"How do you think I'm doing?"

Not that they were bad at their jobs. I just wasn't ready to discuss how I felt. Lord knows, I'm appreciative of what they did. We needed them there. We all appreciated it. It was great to have people to talk to, because the mood in the break rooms was dark sometimes. We were all struggling. But I stayed to myself. I brought my headphones to work, and I would zone out. At times, I ate my lunch in my truck because I didn't want to be around people.

Ultimately, the department started offering group sessions where people on a shift could come together and talk to each other. The department called them debriefs. It was stunning how few people turned out on a shift of maybe sixty people. At the first debrief, there were about six people. I was disappointed in the numbers, and I shared my feelings with a few friends. After what we went through, you would have thought that room would have been filled with officers. But nope, that's not how police operate. We bottle all our shit up inside instead of letting it out. Police are used to being problem solvers. Nothing is allowed to be wrong with us. I talk openly about my counseling and our need for counseling. I wish other officers, and all kinds of other people, would do it, because it helps. I know it helps me.

I have urged other officers to get help. Some do, some don't. I was encouraged after I got a call from my old Capitol Police supervisor. (He also ran the training for my class at the Federal Law Enforcement Training Center in Brunswick, Georgia.) He was there on January 6th. He has since retired. He phoned me after he saw one of my television interviews. He said it was good that I was telling people about counseling, and he was going to talk to somebody about therapy. Another officer sent me a text. It read, "You've convinced me to talk with somebody, because I'm not all right."

I was ready for therapy on January 7. I was like, where is it? I'm ready. I may have been more open to counseling because therapy was normal to me. I had gone through it when I was in middle school, around age thirteen or fourteen. I think my parents saw something in me that they didn't want to turn into something bad. They were concerned about two things. One was anger issues. It wasn't like I was out there getting into fights in school or anything like that. But I was irrational. Sometimes when I got really angry, I'd just walk away. Either I was so upset that I knew I shouldn't say anything, or I was so enraged that I couldn't really talk about what I was feeling. Other times, I would have temper tantrums.

Some things just set me off. I remember one of my triggers was when people called me stupid. I would lose my shit. My little sister called me stupid because she knew it bothered me. I don't know why, but I just hated that word. Also, my mom says I had this protective streak that would get me into trouble. She said if I saw something or believed something was an injustice, it triggered my need to protect people. My mom told me about one time when she wanted to reprimand my sister. She sent me outside because she knew I would get in the way because I always wanted to protect her. Sure enough, I heard her fussing at my sister, and I got so excited that I punched through the glass in the door to get back inside to protect her. I still have that scar on my hand today.

Some people would say I was overreacting. But it wasn't overreacting to me. I had good intentions; I just couldn't control my emotions. Sometimes, I really got out of hand. One time, I thought one of my high school teachers had said something derogatory about my mother. I got so upset that I called her a bitch. Whoa! You would have thought I set the school on fire. The teacher called my mother. My mother called my dad. My dad left his job and came to the school and then my mother arrived right after he got there. Not one of my better days.

So, that was part of the reason for counseling. The other was that I couldn't sit still. I was always doing stuff, and the stuff I was doing wasn't the stuff I was supposed to be doing. It was interfering with my schoolwork and my interactions in class. I was always goofing around. I wasn't paying attention to the teacher. I got in trouble because I wouldn't stop talking. I was trying to be the class clown, the center of attention.

Ms. Johnson, my English teacher, suggested to my parents I get tested. I did and I was diagnosed with attention deficit hyperactivity disorder, ADHD. According to doctors, ADHD is one of the most common childhood disorders. They say it usually shows up in childhood and can continue with you when you become an adult. The doctors prescribed what I later learned was Ritalin. I started taking that every day. I also began counseling.

My counselor, Ms. Horn, had this affected way of talking, like Eartha Kitt in that Eddie Murphy movie *Boomerang*—very proper and British. I'll never forget her accent. I went to counseling at least once a month, sometimes more often, for about two years. I'm sure the counseling helped, but I don't remember that much about it except that I did a lot of talking about my day and about my week.

My dad says what really helped was when he got me into sports. I had grown a lot from elementary to junior high. By the eighth grade, I had shot up to six feet two inches tall. Dad got me into American Athletic Union (AAU) basketball. Our team was the Robinson Panthers. In AAU basketball, you usually play for a local team, but there are teams all over the country. So you travel to play in tournaments in different places. We mostly played in the smaller tournaments in DC, Maryland, and Virginia. You competed in the local tournaments, and, if you were good enough, you would get invited to the big tournaments. We were pretty good, so we played in national tournaments in Texas, New York, Florida, Virginia, Pennsylvania, and California.

One particular game in California was a real turning point for me in terms of my emotional health and the special bond between my dad and me.

Like all drugs, Ritalin has side effects. It can make you feel very awake, excited, alert, and energized, but it can also make you feel agitated and aggressive. Aside from that, no kid wants to wake up every day and take a pill. Adults don't want to do it either, but for a kid, it says something is wrong with you, that you're somehow different or deficient or both, and no kid wants to be either of those. I can't recall exactly how it made me feel, but I know that after a while, I didn't want to take it. I had told my parents I didn't like it, but I had never explicitly asked them to take me off it.

My basketball team was in Compton, California, a suburb of Los Angeles, to play in a summer tournament at Compton High School. I was thirteen. That morning before the game, I pleaded with my dad to let me not take my Ritalin, even if just for one day.

"Dad, I don't need this," I said. "I can do better without this."

He was hesitant. He looked at me and paused. "Okay," he said. "Let's try it today and see how that goes. If it goes well, we'll go day by day after that."

Well, I don't remember my performance as well as my dad does, but he said I was outstanding. He said I played better than I ever had. I had more energy. I played with more intensity and more passion than he had ever seen. Not only that, but I also dunked in the game. I remember that. It was the first time I had ever dunked. I asked my dad about that day. He said, "Anthony"—that's what my family calls me—"you turned into a great athlete after we took you off those pills. The more you got involved in sports, the more temperate you became."

I never took another pill after that day.

But if I hadn't had that counseling when I was a kid, I don't think I would have automatically thought about a therapist after January 6th. Nobody recommended it to me. I just sought it out because I knew from my childhood—and from my divorce—that it could make a difference. It could help heal me.

After my divorce, I was hurt and sad. I felt lost. For one thing, I felt embarrassed. When I got married, I felt like it was going to be forever. I think that's how most people feel. I got married young, twenty-five, but I took it seriously. When I took that marriage vow, that was a deep commitment to me. And I loved my wife. I wanted to build a family with her. My parents had done it. They've been married forty years. So I went into my marriage like that. When it didn't work, I felt like a failure. I felt like I looked stupid, not necessarily because I fucked up but because my marriage fucked up. You know, you work on a marriage, and mine didn't work. I had a lot of anger. "I hate this woman. She's got me looking like a fucking failure." I felt like I needed somebody to talk to, somebody to listen to me and not give me advice. I wasn't afraid to talk to other people, but I didn't know what to say.

Your parents are worried about you. "Are you okay?" You want to say, "Fuck no! I'm not okay!" But you can't say that. So, you don't say anything. You can't talk to your boys, because you just don't know what to say. Your boys are asking, "Are you okay?" You want to say, "No, motherfucker, I am not okay!" You know, you're in the world, and everybody knows you're married. You go to something, some event or just anything, and somebody says, "How is your wife doing?" What are you supposed to say? You just cut the world off.

So I found a therapist. Like I said, I just needed some-body to listen to me. I don't think I told anybody that I was going for counseling. I just went to Google, typed in my zip code, and looked for a therapist near where I lived. I looked at the ratings and reviews and chose one.

You go in there, and you don't even know what to say or where to start. You're confused about everything. But I went and kept going for about ten sessions. Ultimately, my response to the question about how I was doing went from "No, I'm not all right" to "I have my good days, and I have my bad days, but things are trending up." That's a much healthier answer. I was just so mad at her. In the end, I realized she just wasn't the person for me. We weren't right for each other. I got rid of that anger. Once I got rid of that anger, I felt a lot better.

Trying to get back to some sense of normalcy after January 6th, however, was light-years away from any kind of counseling or therapy that I had gone through before. We're talking about a whole new galaxy. None of the other therapy was anything like this. I'm still struggling, still trying to get back to the man I was. I'm a lot better, but I came to realize that recovering from that day is going to be a long process. The hard part is accepting that I will probably never fully heal.

I began individual counseling through the govern-ment's employee assistance program. That was a baby step on the way to recovery. I knew early on that it wouldn't get me to where I needed to be, and my counselor knew it too. She told me that she couldn't give me the help I truly needed. What I needed, she said, was a therapist, and there's a real difference between a counselor and a therapist. Even more, she said, I needed a trauma therapist.

So my lawyer helped me find a great one. He was a former police officer who trained and studied to be a trauma counselor. On my first visit, he asked me a lot of questions to determine where I was mentally. Did I have trouble sleeping, resting, finding peace? Did I have flashbacks? How did certain things make me feel or not feel? That went on for a while. Finally, he looked at his notes and turned to me.

"You have all the signs of classic PTSD," he said.

Post-traumatic stress disorder.

"Okay. So, now what?" I thought.

I knew something was wrong with me—more than the things my counselor and I were discussing. There's a lot going on when you're in that dark place. There is insomnia. The unease. The anger. The flashbacks. Anything could trigger them. I would be walking through the hallways of the Capitol, and January 6th would come flooding back. I could hear the sounds. The metal poles beating against our police shields. The officers screaming for help. The chanting and yelling rioters. People calling us traitors. I could smell that day. The pungent odor of the pepper spray and the fire extinguisher residue. Perspiration. The alcohol on the rioters' breath. I didn't even have to be in the Capitol. I could be watching the news, or in a crowd, or at a store, and I'd be taken back to that day.

Your mind takes you through so much after something like that. I didn't know it before my therapy, but when people go through these situations, it's normal to beat yourself up. You blame yourself. You feel sadness. You feel shame. And it takes a while, and it takes therapy to help you realize that the folks who attacked you bear the responsibility for what you're going through—not you.

Why should we feel sadness when they hurt us? Why do we have to find this strength when we didn't do anything wrong? Our emotions are responding to something that was done to us. You learn that you've got to start putting the blame on the people who did this to us.

Don't blame me. Y'all fuckers are the ones who ought to be ashamed of yourselves. Don't be mad at yourself, bro. You just reacted. They are the ones who did something irresponsible. Why are you sad? We were attacked. Your body is reacting to something that was done to it. That's why it's all right not to be all right. Not to be all right is normal. Then you get hot, you start sweating, and there's nothing you can do about it. It's normal. Your body is reacting. When you are cold, how do you stop shivering? You get warm. How do you stop hurting? You get right. We've got to be kind to ourselves and put the blame where it belongs. It belongs on them!

Let's talk for a minute about PTSD because, unfortunately, I don't think most people really understand it, not even a little bit. Some people don't even think PTSD is real. They think it's something psychiatrists made up, and people like me can use it to get disability. Well, I've got PTSD. I'm working through it, but it's hard. It's painful, and if I didn't have the therapeutic support I have, I don't know if I could make it through this.

First, let's dissect the term. Post-traumatic stress means you're dealing with a horrible incident that happened in your life. Disorder. Think about that. Disorder. You're in an unnatural state. Your life has been turned upside down. Your body is still reacting to a traumatic incident, and you are still dealing with it. It could come at any time and screw up your life. You can't function, or you lose control.

It can show up as depression. It can show up as anger, or it can show up as paranoia. You can't sleep, and you're thinking, what the hell is that? Or you want to be distant. It takes many different forms, so you have to be self-aware.

Going to counseling and therapy does not make you immune to the trials and tribulations of life or of PTSD. However, with the right counseling—and the right counselor or therapist—it will provide you with methods and coping techniques so you will find a way to not stay in that dark place—or not stay too long. Sometimes it may linger on. There's no absolute. It could last for ten minutes or it could last for ten days, but most of the time, it's not with you. Some days, it doesn't bother me at all. It's something that I have to be wary of. I have to be cognizant of that.

Let me give you an example. One day I was out with two or three buddies, and we went to a karaoke spot. It was a fun happening. People were having drinks, talking, laughing. You know, just a good time. A lot of people were bumping into me, not in a bad way. You're in a crowded bar. People are tapping you on the back, "Hey, Harry. What's up?" People who don't know you meet you. "Hey, man, you're a tall guy." Just hanging out.

But then I started getting bothered. I was feeling anxious. It was because I was surrounded by people, and I hadn't been surrounded by that many people since January 6th. What stood out was that I was around friends. It wasn't people who were hostile. Still, I started tensing up. Even though I was around friends, I wanted to turn around and say, "Hey, don't touch me."

Because of my therapy, I was able to say to myself, "Harry, this is bad. You need to get out of here. You don't want to react in a negative way."

I told my friends, "Look, I got to get out of here." They didn't ask me a lot of questions. Maybe an "Are you okay?" But they got it. I went out to my truck and just sat there and started breathing, taking deep breaths. I tried to use my rational brain.

"Hey, Harry, you're with friends. Relax, you're okay." I kept saying that to myself. "I'm okay. I'm okay. I'm okay. I'm okay. I'm okay."

It worked. It didn't get me all the way down, but it worked enough for me to get myself together. I stayed in my car like that until I felt stable enough to drive. I didn't want to be driving and shaking.

What was important was that I was able to think about why I was upset. What are you worried about at this moment? I'm surrounded by people, and I don't know if they're here to hurt me or what. The therapy makes you ask, why are you upset? Am I flashing back to that moment? Usually when you're in a triggered spot, you don't ask why. You just react. Nobody ever thinks about the why.

Once you realize you're in a good space, that these people aren't there to hurt you, you understand that you're overreacting. You figure out how to find healing, how to live with it. It never goes away. You learn how to live with it. You learn how to identify what is happening, and then how to deal with it in a healthy manner. It doesn't make you immune, but it gives you the peace of mind to work through it, so you're not in those dark places as long or as frequently.

I'm still in counseling, but I'm no longer in trauma therapy. No complaints about my trauma therapist, but my needs changed because what I was going through changed. He met me where I was at that time. At one point, I didn't need to talk about the stress of the job. That was fine with me. In fact, it showed progress. Usually I couldn't wait to talk to the therapist about what I was feeling, but it got to the point where I said, "You know, I'm doing well."

9

THE FIGHT IS NEVER OVER

I admit, at times I have felt like, "What is the point?" I'm out here battling in the media, talking with people at events from Portland, Oregon, to Montgomery County, Maryland, about what the Capitol and DC Metropolitan Police and I experienced on January 6th, and I sometimes think, "Why am I doing this? Nothing seems to be happening, and it seems like nothing is going to happen. Shit is just getting worse." Even more than two years after January 6th, there are millions of Americans who actually believe that what we went through that day didn't happen. Some of our elected officials and media repeat and support this lie, even though they know it's not true. You see idiots who keep the lie going, like Tucker Carlson, who, when he had the largest news audience in America, went on Fox News with cherry-picked footage of January 6th.

Too many elected officials and too many Americans have seen the truth on television with their own eyes, but still they will tell you it's a lie.

"It's the liberal media," they say, as though video footage and cell phone images taken by the media *and* the insurrectionists themselves have a political persuasion. There are web pages after web pages, tweets after tweets that continue to spread these vicious lies about what happened that day and what has happened since. They raise up insurrectionists, QAnon conspiracy theorists, and just plain racists as patriots and heroes.

It's insulting because our country, our democracy, was brought so close to the brink of anarchy that General Mark Milley, the highest-ranking military officer in America at that time, had to call a Chinese military leader to assure them that America wasn't coming apart and that Trump wasn't going to launch nuclear missiles against China. It was so insane that Milley, after a call with Nancy Pelosi, in which they both agreed Trump was crazy, called in the group of guys who would be involved with a nuclear missile launch and had them sit in a circle around him and promise that they would not do a damn thing Trump said without consulting with him first. He was not going to have this unhinged madman drag the world into a nuclear war.

But after more than eight hundred days, after officers Michael Fanone, Aquilino Gonell, Daniel Hodges, and I testified before the January 6th Committee, after scores of additional witnesses, including dozens of Republicans and people who worked for Donald Trump testified before the committee and thousands of pages of documents were introduced to show that Donald Trump was responsible for what happened that day, he was still out there. Not only was he out there; he was running for president even as he was facing the possibility of going to jail under a federal indictment for crimes against the United States. The man who tried to steal the country could become the next president. How could we allow that to happen?

It pisses you off. At his campaign rallies, Trump has thousands of Americans standing, cheering, dressed in Trump paraphernalia, waving Trump flags, and giving him, a man who claims to be a billionaire, money. What makes it even worse is that, at some rallies, he has played a recording of the people who attacked us on January 6th singing our national anthem. These are people who are still behind bars for what they did, many of them convicted criminals, and they are celebrated at these rallies. You look around for sanity from certain elected officials, and you get none. I've watched legislators say, "No more Donald Trump," then collapse and turn back into his most loyal supporters. Republicans and journalists have documented how Trump supporters know what he did was wrong. Behind his back, they condemn him. But when the lights are on, they turn back into sycophants and kiss his ring. Author and longtime journalist Mark Leibovich wrote a whole book about it, *Thank You for Your Servitude*. Respected Republican pollster Frank Lutz said he sees it all the time. "They won't say it [in public], but behind his back they think he's a child," Lutz said in an interview. "They're laughing at him." Legendary and Pulitzer Prize-winning Watergate reporter Carl Bernstein named twenty-one Republican senators in an article that he said know Trump is lying and criticize him behind his back, but they won't say so publicly, he said, because they want to hold on to their elected seats.

Even Trump's lapdog, Tucker Carlson, got caught in his giant charade. Carlson has defended Trump at every turn. He knew Trump was lying about the election, even though he and his guests advanced the stolen election bullshit on his show. The truth came out in texts Carlson sent to his colleagues at Fox about Trump's attorney, Sidney Powell, who was running around the country trying to get the election overturned. "Sidney Powell is lying, by the way," he wrote in a November 18, 2020, text to the host of another show. "I caught her. It's insane." He called her "a nut," "poison," a "crazy person," a "lunatic," an "unguided missile" who was "dangerous as hell." But he was willing to go along with it, and he and his buddies at

Fox had her on their shows repeatedly, as well as other people who repeated the stolen election lies.

After a while, Carlson got tired of repeating Trump's lies. He kept up the facade, but this is what he wrote in a text just two days before the insurrection: "We are very, very close to being able to ignore Trump most nights. Truly can't wait."

He knew—no, let me correct that—he knows that Trump is a self-centered, deceitful narcissist who doesn't care for anybody but himself. He knows that Trump certainly doesn't care for this country. "I hate him passionately," he texted his colleagues at Fox. He went on in another text to describe Trump as "a demonic force, a destroyer." But less than a month after these texts, Carlson agreed to travel to Mar-a-Lago for a self-serving interview with Trump. It's all a lie. It's all a charade. This man, who has been proven to be a perpetual liar who will say anything to keep his ratings up, used that same platform to criticize me when it was announced that Fanone, Gonell, Hodges, and I would be testifying before the January 6th Committee.

"Dunn will pretend to speak for the country's law enforcement community, but it turns out Dunn has very little in common with your average cop," Carlson said on his show. "Dunn is an angry, left-wing political activist."

Had Carlson ever met me before he said these things about me? Nope. Did he call me or reach out to me in any way to ask me my opinions or what I might say?

Nope. Did he invite me on to his show after saying those things about me and hearing my testimony so we could talk about what I said? Nope. In fact, Fox made it clear to its producers that they didn't want me or Fanone or any of us on their show.

Carlson, now a proven liar, has not served a day in uniform, whether military or law enforcement, but he has the gall to criticize my service to my country. Carlson and the people like him are liars and will do and say anything to advance their own personal agenda. It's all the more insulting to me and other Capitol Police officers because the first thing we learn about our job is to put our country before ourselves. Yet these people are out there gaining traction.

So, yeah, sometimes you want to just say, "Fuck it."

On the other hand, I have to admit, there is some movement. Hundreds of the people who attacked us on January 6th are in jail, though the guy they called the QAnon Shaman was released early, after being originally sentenced to nearly three and a half years. Some of them are facing long sentences. They will pay a severe price. Violent felony convictions are hard to overcome. Even some of those people with misdemeanor convictions got a wakeup call. But for me and the other officers, that's not enough. Like I said when I testified before the January 6th Committee, "If a hitman is hired, and he kills somebody, the hitman goes to jail. But not only does the hitman go to jail, the person who hired them does. There was an attack carried out on January 6th, and a hitman sent them."

The hitman was Donald Trump, and he needs to answer for his crime.

Do I hope Trump goes to jail for paying to keep his affair with a porn actress quiet? Sure. Do I want Trump to be convicted in Georgia and go to jail for all of the other lies he perpetuated around the election he lost? The answer is yes. Would I like him to go to jail on the federal charges that he held on to top-secret documents and other government property he clearly intended to steal from the government? Definitely. But I have to admit, it won't give me even close to the satisfaction I would get from seeing him tried and convicted for what happened on January 6th. I know it may sound petty, but I personally want Trump to directly pay for what he did to my fellow officers and me.

Police officers lost their lives because of what he did. Their families still hurt and feel the loss of their spouses, siblings, parents, and cousins. Many of us, including me, continue to wrestle with mental trauma from that day. So, yes, I want him to pay for what he did to us. I want my country to recognize the wrong that he did to us and the democracy that we protect.

Only when that happens will I feel truly vindicated. Oh yes, on that day I'm going to celebrate, you can believe that. I'm going to get some extremely special bourbon, and my boys and I are going to toast and laugh and toast and laugh and toast and laugh some more. "Yes, we got that son of a bitch, and he is in jail."

But even as I imagine that day and the pleasure I will feel, I am brought back to earth by a sobering reality. Even if Trump is convicted, even if he can't run for office again, even if he goes to jail, even if everything I want to happen takes place, it won't be over. All those politicians who are rallying around him and his philosophy of hate will still support him when he is behind bars. So will all those self-deluded Americans, QAnon wackos, racists, and conspiracy nuts. Fox News, Newsmax, and so many other right-wing sites will continue to spread lies and advance policies that divide us by looking to blame and demonize one group of Americans so another group of Americans can feel superior.

It's already happening. The Supreme Court over-turned *Roe v. Wade*, so women across the US are once again fighting for the right to a legal abortion. Racism has become so rampant that a member of Congress questioned the loyalty to America of the first Chinese American woman elected to Congress simply because she is Chinese and then said she should be denied intelligence briefings. This is a woman who served her community as a school board member, a member of her local city council, the mayor of her city three times, and a member of the California state assembly.

Because Trump lost in 2020, dozens of state legislatures across the country are making it harder for people to vote. Suddenly, they say they need new rules to protect against voter fraud, even though their own election officials told them that 2020 was the safest election ever. Voting is the foundation of our democracy. It's what sets democracies apart from other forms of government, but they want to make it more difficult—not less—for Americans to exercise their right to choose their government and the policies they want.

They are doing this by putting more restrictions on mail-in voting. They want to shorten the time for early voting, and they want to make it harder for students to vote. At a meeting in Nashville in April 2023, Donald Trump told a bunch of Republicans that if he gets to be president again, he will get rid of all mail-in and early voting. That's right. Americans want to take away other Americans' right to vote because they don't want you to have a say in how your country operates. They don't want you to have the right to protect your freedom.

Then you've got MAGA people and politicians pressuring school systems and libraries to ban books. Ban books in America. In America! This is crazy talk. I kept hearing about it, so I looked it up. According to the American Library Association, between 2020 and 2022, the number of books that were banned from school systems and libraries went from 223 titles to 2,571. That's an increase of over 1,000 percent in just two damn years. And I'm not talking about some new shit that just came out of the woodwork. I'm talking about classic books, like *Catch-22*, *Cat's Cradle*, *The Great Gatsby*, *Beloved*, *Lord of the Flies*, and *To Kill a Mockingbird*.

In Randolph County, North Carolina, the school board banned *Invisible Man* by Ralph Ellison. *Invisible Man* won the National Book Award in 1953. The Library of Congress named it one of the "Books That Shaped America." School board members banned it because the parent of one student complained about it in a twelve-page letter. That's right, one parent. What about the rights of the other parents, the other students? Some board members had never even read it. After they read it, they reversed their decision and put the book back on the shelf.

In Texas, Rep. Matt Krause released a list of about 850 books that he said should be banned because he claimed they "make students feel discomfort" due to their content about race and sexuality. He decided this on his own for all the students and parents in his district, and he wanted school libraries to report whether they had any of the books. This kind of ignorance is not just going on in places like Texas and Florida. We're talking about calls to ban books in thirty-seven of our fifty states. What's so amazing is that school systems are banning books because one parent doesn't want their child to read a particular book. Fine. Don't let your child read the book, but we can't allow one or two people to decide what happens for all the other parents and children.

This is the kind of shit you read about in the history books, about Nazi Germany and how people there banned books. They had big book-burning events that were part of the repression of freedoms that led up to World War II. My maternal grandfather, Eddie Peterson, fought in that damned war. He's now lying in Arlington National Cemetery with the other brave men and women who served this country. He fought for our freedom from such craziness, to protect against such stupidity.

And what books are they most trying to ban? The American Library Association said they are mostly books about Black and LGBTQ people. They want to erase Black people's history and erase LGBTQ people altogether. I'm serious. They want to ban any book that deals with the fact that homosexual people exist in this world and pretend the history of racism and discrimination that African Americans endured didn't happen. And by doing that, they also want to wipe out all of the Black accomplishments that helped make America great, because Black history is American history.

And I think, "Damn! What the fuck?! When will this shit stop?!" It can be pretty damn disheartening. But then I look in the mirror, and I say to myself, "Harry. Stop it! Stop that hopeless bullshit! This is nothing new. It has always been this way. You love this country and what it has become, but it has been this way from the very beginning."

When this country was created, when those great words were written, "All men are created equal," they were not referring to you or even to most of the people reading this book. They were talking about a handful of white men who owned land. They were not referring to women, immigrants, Native Americans, Black people, or even to most white men (who didn't own land), and certainly not to the LGBTQ community. There was no equality for Catholics, Jews, or Muslims.

The Declaration of Independence and the Constitution weren't designed with us in mind. The social world that most of us inhabit in America today, the rights that we exercise daily, have been created and fought for over decades. We have these rights because we pushed and fought and died and suffered to get them, step by step, tragedy by tragedy, defeat by defeat, and victory by victory.

Our problem today is that too many of us have forgotten that truth.

When this country was formed, my ancestors, the African people bought and sold by many of the people who wrote the Declaration of Independence, were mostly enslaved. None of them could vote. None of them had rights. Learning to read and write was a crime. White women had few to no rights. They couldn't vote, much less hold elected office. For decades, they married into near chattel bondage. Up until about thirty years ago, they could be beaten and raped by their husbands without any legal recourse under the label of "domestic violence."

Most immigrants of that day—poor whites—couldn't vote, because they didn't own any land. Most European immigrants were indentured servants—in essence, slaves—until they worked off their time. And the subsequent waves of immigrants, the Irish, Italians, Puerto Ricans, and Mexicans, fought through legal and ad hoc discrimination and prejudice to make the lives they have now. Every one of us fought like hell to make America a place where those words ring true for us. And we have to keep fighting because when we stop, we end up with a government run by people like Donald Trump and the people who suck up to him.

Every group—women, Blacks, immigrants, Asians, Muslims, Native Americans—has a story to tell about how we came from being oppressed to a place where we can walk in the sun without fear and with the protection of this great nation. It was a mere fifty-four years ago that we lived in an America where gay men and women were hiding in "closets." There were no openly gay men and lesbians in Congress, no openly married gay couples raising families and living their lives, no openly LGBTQ teachers and professors in our schools and universities, running corporations and small businesses, entertaining and thrilling us with their talents in music, film, art, and theater. They weren't open within their own families. They didn't dare let their identity be known. The penalty was prison, shame, and total ostracism from their families, from their communities, and from the ability to make a living.

Our culture ridiculed and demeaned them. They were told—no, we were all told—that they were freaks, sexual deviants, sinful, and unnatural. They were made to feel ashamed for being who they were. Men married women and women married men, not out of love but to hide their sexuality. That was particularly true if they were in high-profile jobs or wanted to pursue public office. It was a crime in most states for men and women to engage in sex with people of the same gender, and the State Department added gay men and lesbians to the list of people it considered security risks.

But on June 28, 1969, the patrons and employees of a gay nightclub in New York City had enough of being brutalized by police and being ridiculed and abused by society. They fought back, and the movement for equality for LGBTQ Americans began. It was called the Stonewall Riots. That day, New York Police, armed with an arrest warrant, raided the Stonewall Inn, an unlicensed bar in New York City's Greenwich Village that was popular among the LGBTQ community. It was unlicensed because the New York State Liquor Authority penalized and shut down establishments that served alcohol to suspected LGBTQ individuals. It claimed that the mere gathering of homosexuals was "disorderly." So, police routinely raided the club and beat and arrested patrons and employees. Similar situations were going on in other major urban cities. Cops entered the club that night; roughed up patrons; and, finding bootlegged alcohol, arrested thirteen people, including employees. They also arrested people for violating the state's gender-appropriate clothing statute. Female officers took suspected cross-dressing men and women into the bathroom to check their sex.

That night, the gay community decided enough was enough. For six days, patrons and other Greenwich Village residents organized into activist groups, demanding the right to live openly regarding their sexual orientation, without fear of being arrested. The new activist organizations concentrated on confrontational tactics, and, within months, three newspapers were established to promote rights for gay men and lesbians. They had thrown down the gauntlet, and after that everything changed.

On the first anniversary of the Stonewall Riots, the nation's first gay pride parades were held in four cities— New York, Chicago, San Francisco, and Los Angeles. (Pride events are now held worldwide every year.) Three years later, the American Psychological Association's board of trustees voted to remove homosexuality as a mental disorder from its diagnostic manual. Four years later, Harvey Milk became the first openly gay man elected to public office when he was selected by voters to the San Francisco Board of Supervisors. In his first year, he sponsored a bill banning discrimination in public accommodations, housing, and employment based on sexual orientation. The bill was signed into law after the supervisors passed it eleven to one.

Skip ahead to 2020, when the Supreme Court made it illegal to discriminate against LGBTQ people in the workplace and in public accommodations. Five years earlier, the court ruled that women and men could legally marry their partners regardless of gender. Today, members of the LGBTQ community work openly at the highest levels of government, science, and industry.

But for every step forward for that community, there was pushback. For example, the same year that Milk pushed through his anti-discrimination bill in San Francisco, Florida, led by singer and anti–gay rights activist Anita Baker, repealed the state law prohibiting discrimination against people for their sexual orientation. The state also approved a law that prohibited gay adoption. Less than a year after Milk was elected to office, he was gunned down by a former supervisor because he was gay. When the AIDS epidemic struck, initially, the gay community was vilified by politicians and religious leaders. It was called the "gay plague." One of the nation's leading religious leaders, a man who helped elect Ronald Reagan president, said, "AIDS is not just God's punishment for homosexuals; it is God's punishment for the society that tolerates homosexuals."

In 1993, President Bill Clinton created a policy that allowed gays in the military to be booted out if their sexual orientation became public. An estimated thirteen thousand people were expelled from the US Armed Forces under the policy, until President Barack Obama repealed it in 2011. In 1996, Congress passed, and Clinton signed, the Defense of Marriage Act, which stated that marriage was only between one man and one woman. It also denied gay couples the right to file joint taxes. It excluded them from the protections of the Family Medical and Leave Act, and it blocked surviving spouses from accessing veterans' benefits, among other things.

Four years later, the Supreme Court ruled that the Boy Scouts of America could bar gay Scouts and leaders from being members. It would be thirteen years before the Boy Scouts lifted the ban in 2013. That same year, the Supreme Court ruled the Defense of Marriage Act was unconstitutional. It's a new day for LGBTQ people. Many heterosexual Americans fought hard alongside the LGBTQ community for them to have those rights. But we now know it's not over. Some states still are trying to take away their rights and to demonize them. When I look through the history books or talk to my parents or my grandparents and their friends, I am amazed at how different a country we are from just a few decades ago. We once lived in a country where women were denied the right to vote simply because they were women. Women only got that right in 1920, after marching, being beaten, and being jailed and ridiculed. They won it forty-seven years after they first petitioned Congress.

Even with the vote in hand, more than forty years later, in 1962, fewer than four of every one hundred representatives in Congress were women, even though women made up 50 percent of the population. Today, that number is still comparatively low, but women now make up 28 percent of Congress. Today, women are routinely governors, ambassadors, and presidential cabinet members. What president today would dare have a cabinet that didn't include women? Still, for so very, very long, married women were near slaves in their own homes. It wasn't until 1981 that the Supreme Court got rid of a Louisiana state law that said the husband is "head and master" of the house and has total control of any property that the couple owned.

Women could be refused employment because they were women. They could be fired because they were women. They could be refused entrance to college because they were women. There were no girls' or women's sports in high school or college like there were for boys and men, because nobody made the schools do it. Not that long ago, most institutions wouldn't give women credit cards without asking them questions like whether they had children or were going to have children or whether they had a husband.

If a woman was single—she could have been divorced or widowed—she might be required to bring a male relative with her to cosign for a credit card because, in essence, her salary didn't count. From the inception of the Constitution until about thirty years ago, men beating their wives was viewed as a family matter, out of the purview of the criminal justice system. A man could beat, rape, or do damn near anything else he wanted to his wife short of murder without repercussions, as long as she didn't press charges.

The tide began to change in the 1970s, and from 1984 to 1988, police in state after state began responding differently to abuse by spouses. Police started to treat "domestic violence" the same as fights between strangers, which resulted in a dramatic increase in the arrests and prosecutions of men for abusing their spouses. That change was codified with the passage of the federal Violence Against Women Act in 1994.

Not long ago, we lived in a country in which men and women were denied employment and entry into restaurants, restrooms, public transportation, movie theaters, hotels, public schools, the nation's colleges and universities, and educational institutions they supported with their tax money because of the color of their skin or their religion. Yes, Harvard, Yale, Princeton, Columbia, and many other colleges and universities had quotas for how many Jews they would admit. They wouldn't, however, allow Jews in fraternities, clubs, or other organizations. Some hotels explicitly advertised "no Hebrews."

It's hard for many of us to imagine a country in which that policy applied to Black, Brown, and Asian people all over America. It happened so often that African Americans came up with the "Green Book" to tell them which hotels would house them, which restaurants would feed them, and where they could stop for gas. Those policies existed for decades, and not just in the South. My mother remembers that time. She told me the story of how her very light-skinned mother, whom the waiter initially thought was white, was refused service in a Baltimore restaurant when servers saw her obviously Black child.

Then she told me about the time when her parents, my grandparents, had planned this glorious summer vacation for her and her siblings:

It was the summer of 1970, the year before I graduated from high school. We were living in

Lanham [Maryland]. I was the oldest. So, it was me, my two younger sisters, and my brother. My parents purchased a brand-new car just before the trip, a brown Chrysler station wagon. We packed up the car and headed west to Chicago. My older sister lived in Chicago, and we wanted to visit her. We spent a day or two there, and then headed out.

Our final destination was to visit an aunt, my father's sister, who lived in San Pedro, California. My dad had called and made a reservation at a hotel in Oklahoma because that was a long drive. I don't remember the name of the hotel, but he got a reservation because he wanted to be sure we had a place to stay when we got there. But when we got there, the clerk at the front desk saw my father's Black face, and he said there were no vacancies. He told my dad, "You can park out there in the parking lot tonight." That's where we slept that night. Two adults, a teenager, and two younger children. I don't know how we did it.

There was an America not long ago in which some Americans created and held on to legal documents that allowed them to discriminate against other Americans. They were called restrictive covenants. They were legal, written contracts that kept certain people from owning or renting a home or living in a certain neighborhood unless they were white. Typically, the contracts read like this: "No part of said property nor any portion thereof shall be for said term of fifty years occupied by any person not of the Caucasian race. It being intended thereby to restrict the use of said property for said period of time against the occupancy of owners or tenants of any portion of said property for residence or other purpose by people of the Negro or Mongolian race."

That one was from a community in St. Louis. Here's one from a house built in 1950 in the El Cerritos community in San Diego: "(15) That neither shall lots nor portions thereof or interest therein shall ever be leased, sold, devised, conveyed to or inherited or be otherwise acquired by or become property of any person other than of the Caucasian Race. (16) That neither said lot nor any portion thereof shall ever be lived upon or occupied by any person other than of the Caucasian Race strictly in the capacity of servants or employees."

One in Minneapolis in 1910 read, "Premises shall not at any time be conveyed, mortgaged or leased to any person or persons of Chinese, Japanese, Moorish, Turkish, Negro, Mongolian or African blood or descent."

This was our America until fifty-five years ago, and even today some unenforceable covenants still exist. Add to these private contracts the practices and rules by our own federal government that further segregated Black and Brown people and excluded them from buying homes in certain neighborhoods in more than two hundred cities. It was called "redlining." Federal housing officials refused to lend money to African Americans to live in white neighborhoods while also making it difficult for them to get loans in their own neighborhoods. My mother remembers that too.

She told me how when she was in the ninth grade, her parents, my grandparents, were looking to buy a house. My grandparents, accompanied by the real estate agent, initially wanted to look at developments and neighborhoods in Bowie, Maryland. "The agent would steer them away from Bowie, which was then pretty much all white. He would say, 'Oh, we can do better than that over here.' Then they would show them something in Glenarden, because a lot of Black people were moving into Glenarden. They ended up buying a house in a new development called Timora Woods," which is now called Lanham, Maryland. After legal fights and protests, racial housing discrimination was outlawed in 1968.

The forty-hour workweek, the minimum wage, food that doesn't kill us, drugs that don't kill us, restrictions on child labor, government requirements to keep us safe on our jobs, access for people with disabilities, the guarantee of clean water, health care for the elderly, health care for the poor, rules for safer cars, rules for safer homes. At one point, none of this existed.

I apologize for my meandering history lesson, but I hash out all this stuff to remind you that the America we live in today is not the America we inherited from our founders or even our forefathers a lifetime ago. It's the one we built by voting, by protesting, by agitating, by demanding, by being arrested, by getting into "some good trouble, necessary trouble," as civil rights icon, former member of Congress, and my hero, John Lewis, would say.

We got these rights by fighting, not on some faraway battlefield but right here at home.

In my anger and my grief over what happened on January 6th, I have, at times, forgotten that very important lesson that you, the American people, teach me every day as I stand my post at the Capitol. Ensuring and protecting our rights is continuous. Making this country better for all of us never ends. We fight not one day but every day.

Unfortunately, too many of us forgot that important lesson, and we took our eyes off the ball in 2016 and allowed Donald Trump to be elected. We elected a Black president twice, and we assumed we were going to take the next step by electing the first female president. We figured nobody would vote for a bombastic, bigoted, narcissistic hotel owner who even Republican Party leaders didn't like. Consequently, Black men and women didn't vote in 2016 like they had voted in previous presidential elections. The turnout in 2016 was the lowest among African Americans for a presidential election than in the previous twenty years. Progressive women didn't come out. So Trump, the man who bragged on a video recording that when it came to women, he liked to "grab them by the pussy," won more women's votes than Hillary Clinton did.

We didn't vote, so we ended up with Donald Trump and everything that came with him. Racists and right-wing extremist groups had a friend in the White House, and they came out of the holes they were hiding in—the Proud Boys, the Oath Keepers, the Three Percenters. Eight months after his inauguration, hundreds of white nationalists, neo-Nazis, and far-right extremists marched with torches through the University of Virginia campus in Charlottesville, Virginia. One of their members backed his car over a bunch of counterprotesters and killed a woman. When Trump was asked about her death, he said there were "good people on both sides." Trump placed a travel ban on six predominantly Muslim countries. He withdrew the United States from the all-important 2015 Paris Accord to reduce climate change. He began placing conservative justices on the Supreme Court. This was all in his first year.

Ultimately, he placed three far-right justices on the Supreme Court, who immediately, with their three other conservative colleagues, eliminated *Roe v. Wade* and women's right to choose. While we blinked, the March for Life people held steady. Every year for nearly forty years, they have come to Washington forty thousand strong to roll back *Roe v. Wade*. They got what they wanted. So the lesson for me, and I think for all Americans who want to protect their freedoms, is to be diligent, to be steadfast. We cannot falter. We cannot flinch. We must honor our heroes and sheroes who created the America we live in by continuing their work. When I think about Trump and his madness these days, I don't feel despair. I am fired up. I am committed to putting that son of a bitch in jail and fighting off all the minions who carry his poisonous, destructive message.

Part of my inspiration is the men and women I fought with on January 6th. They never backed down. I remember how, while we were fighting against the insurrectionists, sometimes the pepper and bear spray would be too much, so officers would come inside and clear their eyes with water. But as soon as they got a second breath, they rushed back to the front. They never stopped. They never quit.

I promise I will do the same. I will always be standing my ground.

EPILOGUE

People say once you've made it through a life-and-death experience, every day is a good day. Even a bad day is a good day, because you know what it's like to almost not have a day at all. There's a lot of truth to that. I loved living before, but I cherish every moment more now after going through January 6th. When I hug my daughter, my parents, my siblings, and my friends, I pull them just a tad closer. It's special. Everything around me is special: the air, the music, the trees, my truck, the rain, the snow, the birds. You name it, and I just appreciate it all a little more. That new feeling, though, is about more than being alive. You have to make it *through* that experience. You have to make it to the other side of that moment.

Many times, people don't make it through. Unfortunately, a lot of people have physically survived terrible incidents—wars, debilitating accidents, diseases, catastrophes—but the horror and trauma of those events have continued to haunt them. For some of us, there are real physical injuries that have changed who we are, what we can do, and how we see ourselves and the world around us.

"I survived, but I'm in a wheelchair. What is life for me now?"

"I survived, but I lost an arm. I lost a leg. I lost a foot. Can I go back to my old career? I'm blind. I'm deaf. Who am I now?"

It's hard to try to accept that and reshape your life. And then, will the people around you accept it? Does your spouse accept it? Your partner? Your children? Your friends?

For some of us, the mental anguish of such moments is unbearable. We can't shake it. It stays with us, sometimes for years. Sometimes forever. Some of us lean on alcohol and drugs to get by, which just makes matters worse. We don't go to therapy, or we can't get therapy because we can't afford to pay for it. Oh yes, that's true for a lot of Americans.

I'm talking about everyday, working Americans who can't afford treatment. I'm not necessarily talking about poor people. I'm talking about people with jobs, in some cases good jobs. The copay is so deep they can't afford to keep it up.

I understand the fight to hold on to your sanity or to reclaim it. I struggled, and I still struggle, but fortunately not as much. But I found if you can make it through the fight to stay alive, and then make it through the consequences of being so close to death, life takes on new meaning. The world becomes an even more beautiful place. You're here. You're alive. You've got one more chance to make things better.

Every day is a good day, even the bad days.

A lot of people helped me to get here. I've already talked about many of them, fellow cops, those with the Capitol Police and all those hundreds from other departments who came to the Capitol after January 6th to help talk us through our trauma. I wasn't always the most receptive guy, I know that, but I don't want them to ever think I don't appreciate everything they did for us. I couldn't have made it through without the therapists, my family, my close friends, and the thousands of people who sent me letters and cards when I was being brutalized in the press just for telling the truth or when I was getting tweets and social media shit from the MAGA people. The positive feedback helped me so much. Then there is my James Madison University crew. They were there for me. They would hit me up on Facebook or Instagram or through text messages. Thank you.

I want to say more about a special group of friends who helped me in a unique way, but first I need to tell you

I love being a dad. Probably more than anybody, my daughter, Daphne, kept me grounded. While I was going through everything related to January 6th—therapy, testifying in the Oath Keepers' trial, testifying before the January 6th Committee, being attacked by Tucker Carlson, and receiving death threats by the hundreds—my pretty little twelve-year-old was the one thing that kept me grounded. I was just one thing to her: Dad.

She didn't know anything about January 6th. I wasn't a hero to her because of something I did that day. I didn't get any props for being on television. I was just Dad, and because I was Dad, I was her hero, her friend, the person she shared with. She's got eyes like mine, and when she flashes those eyes at me and gives me that big smile, I just fall in love repeatedly. And because she doesn't know anything about January 6th, we never talk about it. Instead, we're in the car riding down the highway, and she's telling me about the latest TikTok trends, and I have to be present whether I'm really that interested or not. I have to pay attention. I have to engage.

"Dad, Dad, my friend has her own YouTube channel."

"Really?!" I say, trying to sound so excited about her friend's channel. "Wow, that's nice, honey."

"Yeah, and she has six hundred subscribers."

"Wow. That's a lot. What's on her channel?"

Or she's watching something on her phone and suddenly she'll say, "Daddy, look, look!"

And I've got to look. Or we could be driving down the street and she'll say, "Wow, look at that red car. My friend Josie's mom has a red car, and she drives fast."

Or I ask, "So, what did you do in school today?"

"We did math."

"What kind of math?"

"You know, math math."

"No, I don't know. Tell me about it."

This could go on for twenty minutes, and I'm having fun. I'm not thinking about anything related to January 6th. I'm talking to this wonderful creature that I helped bring into the world. I love how I helped create something, that the outcome of her life is dependent on my role as her father raising her. She's hungry. She's cold. Her tooth falls out. Obviously, it isn't about me at all, which is great.

After January 6th, we were working twelve-hour shifts, seven days a week. So, I was tired after I got off, and I was going through a lot. I was returning to the crime scene every day, and I was feeling that. I was jumpy and closed off. It got a little dicey at times. One day I got a package on my doorstep, and it got me nervous. Was it a bomb? Was it anthrax or ricin or some other dangerous shit?

I was so relieved and touched when I opened it. It was a care package: herbal teas, bath bombs, and stress-release supplements, like ashwagandha. It was great to be thought of in that capacity. But after I got off work at the end of a shift, everybody would want to talk to me about how I was feeling. "Are you okay?" I appreciated the concern, but it got annoying after a while. Sometimes I would avoid people because I didn't want to talk about it. I didn't want them to ask me if I was okay. I would tell people, "I don't want to talk about it. I will tell you when I'm ready to talk."

I was okay talking to the media, but I didn't know how to talk to my friends and family about it. I didn't mind being short with the media. I didn't mind being angry with the media, because I didn't really care how I came off when I was talking to reporters. My friends and family, though, they knew me as the fun-loving happy guy. I didn't want to have that tone with them.

My boys and I didn't have those interactions, you know, talking about January 6th or how I was feeling. They would just call me up and say, "Harry, we're going to have a bourbon tasting tonight at R. J.'s." It sounds fancy, but we're just drinking it down. We were talking about rap, sports, hip-hop, TV shows, the barbershop. We would sit around with cigars, music playing. I didn't have to talk about January 6th because they didn't bring it up.

Those are my guys, R. J., James, Morgan, Shawn, and Joe. These are guys I can count on. If my tire is flat, I can call them, no matter what time. "Hey, can you come and scoop me up?" They are there when I need them, and I am there when they need me. We lift each other up.

Not long ago, we were in a group chat and Joe was like, "I'm throwing some burgers on the grill." The next thing you know, we are all at Joe's house. That was 5 p.m. Before I knew it, it was 11 p.m. We like to chill and be in each other's company. R. J., James, and Joe are fathers too. Our kids are about the same age. Sometimes we talk about how to navigate tough issues with children. James is the only one who is together with the mother of his child, so the others, we talk about navigating life as single fathers. We talk about our feelings. It's not therapy, but it helps. We lean on each other.

We all collect bourbon. We each have a hundred-plus bottles of bourbon on our bars. On the second Saturday of every month, a liquor store in Montgomery County does an allocated bourbon drop, where they release rare and hard-to-find bourbons. We will go out at two or three in the morning and wait outside for the store to open. That may sound crazy as hell to somebody, but you do it for fellowship. Russell's Reserve 13, I got it for $69, but you can resell it for $300. Stagg Jr., I got that for $79 and it goes for over $300 online. Pappy Van Winkle can range from $1,000 to more than $3,000 a bottle. Old Forester Birthday Bourbon is no less than $1,200. I got a bottle of Old Carter, and it is really hard to find. You are not going to drink a bottle of that rare bourbon every day, but collecting it is fun, and every now and then, we'll share from a bottle.

Going through what I have gone through has really awakened me to the power of the media and a couple of subjects that are dear to me: better policing and mental health for men. I have been talking with a friend about the idea of launching a podcast. I got the idea after watching LeBron James. He has a podcast called *The Shop*. It's based on the idea of going to a barbershop. (In the Black community, the barbershop is where people go not just to get their hair cut or styled but also to have lively discussions about what's going on in their neighborhoods and in the world. Some people go to the barbershop even when they don't need a haircut. A lot of Black people like to chop it up. It's therapeutic.)

In LeBron's podcast, which is video too, he and his boys, which can include women, are sitting around in barber chairs talking about sports, but they also talk about music or just life. I want to do the same thing with Black police officers. I want to talk about policing through our eyes. Every other week it seems there's a video of an encounter of a Black person with police. I want to bring transparency to that process that people can see. How did this encounter happen? Why did it happen? What is the normal police procedure, and did this interaction go outside the norms? Was there a better way this encounter could have happened? Maybe I can get some prosecutors to come on the show to talk about, for example, how Black women are locked up longer than white men for killing somebody. Maybe we look at law enforcement practices in Europe, or wherever, to get a better handle on this subject. I think we can fix this shit. We won't fix the issue of bad policing by having good police officers leave.

The other thing I'm thinking of doing is creating a nonprofit on mental health. I want to call it MENtal Health. It will be geared toward men because we don't take care of ourselves. I want to focus on fathers, gay men, and men of color—men who are the most vulnerable because they have stigmas attached to their lives. I have to do a lot of research on that.

I'm always tweeting out the phrase "Be the change you want to see in the world." Many people think it came from Mahatma Gandhi, but it didn't. It is from *The Love Project Way*, written in 1970 by Arleen Lorrance, when she was a high school teacher in Brooklyn, New York. That phrase is important, and it means a lot to me. Like I said before, I've been given a new lease on life, another chance to make a difference, and that's what I want to do.

Be the change I want to see in the world.

ACKNOWLEDGMENTS

To my lovely daughter Daphne. I love you. Mom and Dad, Mrs. Joyce and Mr. Harry L. Dunn, my sisters Lisa, Crystal, Cristen, and Janice. Love y'all. To my cousin Jarryd and Trent, my brother from another mother, and "The Fellas." Time to pour a healthy one!

To Erin Smith, Serena Lienbengood, Sandra Garza, Mrs. Gladys Sicknick. My heart is with you always.

To Monique, Jamie, Alesha, my "petty" and "wyld" friends. Appreciate y'all more than you know. Thanks to the entire Capitol Division of the Capitol Police, our leader, Inspector Thomas Loyd, and a huge thank you to the First Responder Unit section two. Thanks for having my "Six."

To the congressional community, whether you're an intern, a senior staffer, a doorkeeper, a groundskeeper, or a cafeteria worker. To all the people at the Architect of the Capitol, the Office of Attending Physicians, and the Capitol Visitors Center. Thank you for your support. "Cram" to Capitol Police officer Eugene Goodman. To Captain Carneysha Mendoza. Thanks, I needed that hug. Shout-out to Recruit Officer Class161. The finishing line is getting closer. To the Lienbengood Wellness Center. You helped me before, and you continue to help me more than you know, and I am thankful.

To Speaker Nancy Pelosi. Thank you for EVERY-THING. To my personal congressman, Rep. Jamie Raskin. You motivate me with your passion. Congressman Eric Swalwell. Thank you. To Congressman Benny Thompson, Congresswoman Liz Cheney, and the entire January 6th Committee and staff. Thank you for your tireless work.

To Nicolle Wallace and Joy Reid at MSNBC. Thank you for not only seeing a story but also for seeing a person. To Michelle Cumbo, Jamie Gangel, Danny Silva, Whitney Wild, Brandi Buchman, and Mike Valerio. Thank you for always offering me a listening ear. Thanks to Pierre Thomas for your commitment to tell my story right.

To Kirsten Neuhaus at Ultra Literary Agency. Helen Dooley at Tandem Sports + Entertainment and Meredith Geisler. What a ride it's been, huh? Thank you! My attorneys, David Laufman and Mark Zaid. Thank you for your care and guidance and helping me through the thorny legal issues. I don't know how I could have done any of this without you. To Ron Harris. We did it! Let's make some more magic. What do you say?

To my James Madison University community. Thank you for your unwavering support. Go Dukes!

To my #Thirstfordemocracy friends. Thank you all. Hey DGFL, my fantasy football league. I'm coming for my trophy. To those who I have confided in, who have lent an ear, to all who provided and continue to provide messages or thoughts of well wishes, you really have helped me make it to this point and you inspire me to keep going. Thanks to Malaika Adero and Robert Scott Adams for your contributions.

Finally, to my brothers and sisters Michael Fanone, Danny Hodges, Aquilino Gonell, Caroline Edwards, and Byron Evans. Thank you for refusing to be silent. Thank you for being the incredible people you are and thank you for your friendship. I'll be there for you anytime you call. Anyone I have left off, please charge it to my head and not my heart.

Love.